Drive-Ins of Route 66

Second Edition

Michael Kilgore

Copyright © 2022 by Michael Kilgore

All Rights Reserved.

Published by Neon Jukebox, Denver, Colorado

Except for Fair Use, no part of this book may be reproduced in any form by any means without the express permission of the author. (That permission is typically easy to get if you ask.) This includes, but is not limited to, reprints, excerpts, photocopying, recording, interpretive dance, semaphore, Aldis lamp, Morse code, or any other way of reproducing this book.

For permission requests, or just to say "Hello," please send an email to mkilgore@carload.com.

Published in the United States

ISBN: 978-1-7333655-6-7

Library of Congress Control Number: 2022901330

First printing, February 2022

Table of Contents

Introduction	1
A Brief History of Drive-Ins	3
A Brief History of Route 66	15

Illinois

Cicero	
Bel-Air Drive-In	23
Countryside	
66 Drive-In	26
Romeoville	
Bel-Air Drive-In	28
Joliet	
Hilltop Drive-In	29
Pontiac	
Pontiac / Star Chief Drive-In	31
Bloomington	
Phil-Kron / Bloomington Drive-In	33
Lincoln	
Bennis Auto Vue Drive-In	35
Lincoln Drive-In	36
Springfield	
Springfield Drive-In	38
Bonus: (Kerasotes) Twin Drive-In	40
66 Drive-In	41
Green Meadows / Route 66 Drive-In	43
Litchfield	
Sky View Drive-In	45
Mount Olive	
Sunset Drive-In	47
Pontoon Beach	
Bel-Air Drive-In	49
Collinsville	
Mounds / Falcon Drive-In	51
East St. Louis	
Shop City Drive-In	52
Intermission:	
Route 66 paths through greater St. Louis	54

Missouri

St. Louis	
Thunderbird Drive-In	57
Broadway Drive-In	58
Jennings	
North Drive-In	60
Crestwood	
66 Park-In	62
Des Peres	
Manchester Drive-In	65
Bridgeton	
Skyline Drive-In	67
St. Ann	
Airway Drive-In	69
St. Ann 4-Screen Drive-In	71
Overland	
Holiday Drive-In	75
Sappington	
Ronnie's Drive-In	76

Valley Park
- I-44 Drive-In — 78

Sullivan
- Grande Drive-In — 80

Cuba
- 19 Drive-In — 82

Rolla
- Rolla Drive-In — 84

St. Robert
- Woodlane Drive-In — 86

Lebanon
- Ski-Hi Drive-In — 89

Marshfield
- Skyline Drive-In — 90

Springfield
- Holiday Drive-In — 92
- Springfield Drive-In — 93
- Sunset Drive-In — 94

Carthage
- Sunset Drive-In — 96
- 66 Drive-In — 98

Webb City
- Webb City Drive-In — 101

Joplin
- Crest Drive-In — 102
- Tri-State Drive-In — 104

Intermission:
- Autoscopes — 105

Kansas

Baxter Springs
- Twilite Drive-In — 109

Intermission:
- Common Denominators — 111

Oklahoma

Miami
- Tri-State / Sooner Drive-In — 113
- Sooner Drive-In — 114

Vinita
- Lariat Drive-In — 116

Claremore
- Rogers Drive-In — 117

Tulsa
- Hi-Way 66 / 11th Street Drive-In — 118
- Airview Drive-In — 120
- Modernaire / Admiral Twin Drive-In — 122
- Apache Drive-In — 124
- Sheridan Drive-In — 125
- Riverside Drive-In — 127
- Bellaire Drive-In — 128

Sapulpa
- Tee-Pee Drive-In — 129

Bristow
- Pirate Drive-In — 132

Davenport
- Rig Drive-In — 134

Edmond
- Woodstock / Edmond Drive-In — 136
- Sundown Drive-In — 137

Oklahoma City
- N'eastern 66 / 66 / Cinema 66 Drive-In — 138
- Fair Park Drive-In — 139
- Northwest Highway Drive-In — 141

Table of Contents

North Penn Twin Drive-In	142
Twilight Gardens Drive-In	144
Cinema 70 Drive-In	146
Circle / Cinema C Drive-In	147

Bethany
Lake Air Drive-In	148

El Reno
El Reno / Squaw Drive-In	150

Weatherford
40 West / 66 West Twin Drive-In	153

Clinton
Clinton Drive-In	156

Elk City
66 Drive-In	158

Erick
Bearcat Drive-In	159

Intermission:
Concession Stand Evolution 161

Texas

Shamrock
Pioneer Drive-In	165

McLean
Derby Drive-In	167

Amarillo
Trail Drive-In	169
Skyway Drive-In	172
Tascosa Drive-In	173
Twin Drive-In	176
Palo-Duro Drive-In	178
Sunset Drive-In	179

Intermission:
The Trail That Wasn't 180

New Mexico

Tucumcari
County / No Name Drive-In	183
Canal Drive-In	185

Santa Rosa
Sky-Ranch Drive-In	187

Albuquerque
Terrace Drive-In	188
Wyoming Drive-In	191
Tesuque Drive-In	192
Duke City Drive-In	194
Cactus Drive-In	196
San Jose / Tri-C / Route 25 Drive-In	198
Sunset Drive-In	200
66 Drive-In	201

Grants
Sahara Drive-In	204

Milan
Trails Drive-In	206

Gallup
Zuni Drive-In	208
Yucca Drive-In	210

Intermission:
Route 66 Motel Neon 211

Arizona

Holbrook
Western Star Drive-In	217
66 Drive-In	219

Winslow
Tonto Drive-In	220

Flagstaff
Mt. Elden Drive-In	223

Kingman		Montclair	
Sage Drive-In	225	Valley Drive-In	245
Intermission:		La Verne	
Wigwam Motels	226	Mt. Baldy Drive-In	248

California

		Azusa	
		Azusa Foothill Drive-In	250
Needles		Duarte	
Sands Drive-In	229	Big Sky Drive-In	252
Barstow		Arcadia	
Skyline Drive-In	231	Edwards Drive-In	254
Lenwood		Pasadena	
Bar-Len Drive-In	234	Hastings Drive-In	257
Victorville		Los Angeles	
Joshua Drive-In	236	Los Feliz Drive-In	259
Bonus: Balsam Drive-In	238	Gilmore Drive-In	260
San Bernardino		Pacific / Pico Drive-In	263
Mt. Vernon Drive-In	240	Olympic Drive-In	266
Rialto			
Foothill Drive-In	242	Bonus Gallery	269
Fontana		Acknowledgments	273
Bel-Air Drive-In	244	Index/About the Author	277

Introduction

Welcome to the expanded, revised second edition of *Drive-Ins of Route 66*.

I've learned a lot since the publication of the first edition in September 2019. More information from more contributors means better details and improved accuracy. More photos make this second edition more attractive to read. And a small shift in emphasis, toward telling the stories of the drive-ins and their people, should make it more fun to read.

This should be (knock on wood) a complete list of every drive-in theater that was ever active within three miles of US 66 or its official alternates. Versions of 66 that were decommissioned before a nearby drive-in could open don't count. (I'm thinking of you, Santa Fe NM.) Ditto for drive-ins that opened after US 66 was decommissioned, such as the I-270 in Florissant MO.

Before we get to the trip from Chicago to L. A., there will be a couple of short chapters, one on the history of drive-ins in general, and the other on the history of Route 66. As we pass state borders on our journey, we'll pause for intermissions — interesting topics tangentially related to drive-ins and Route 66.

(By the way, when I refer to a drive-in or other cinema house, I use the "theater" spelling, which is more common in today's American English. A century ago, "theatre" was more common, so quotes often use that spelling. Whichever way it's spelled, I meant to do that.)

Important disclaimer: Despite my best efforts, probably at least one detail in this book will turn out to be wrong. There are so many dates and names from so many sources that it's unlikely that they're all perfect.

There's also a lot of stuff missing from the drive-in entries in this book. Though the pool of information sources grew since the first book, there are still more that I couldn't get to. If you know about something that should have been included, please drop me a line.

Now sit back and relax as we get ready to travel 2400 virtual miles and decades into the past. This should be fun!

Michael Kilgore
Carload.com

Find a good place to park - the show's going to start soon! 2021 photo by the author of the Litchfield IL Sky-View.

A Brief History of Drive-Ins

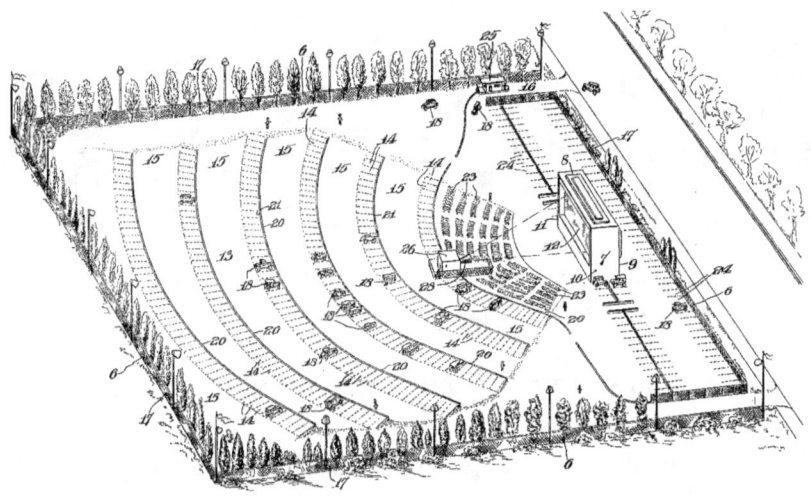

One of the drawings from Richard Hollingshead Jr.'s original drive-in theater patent.

Although silent-movie "drive-ins" had previously popped up now and then, their history really starts with inventor Richard Hollingshead Jr., who got the first drive-in theater patent on June 1, 1933. What he really invented wasn't the outdoor theater — it was the drive-in ramp, which angled each car up to better point at the screen. You might also give him credit for most viewing fields' clamshell design, shown above.

The Shaky Start

Hollingshead's first location, which opened June 6, 1933, near Camden NJ, was not a success. It was popular enough, but as with most 1930s drive-ins, its main

A front-seat view of the first drive-in theater in Camden NJ, as it appeared in *Motion Picture Herald*.

problem was sound — no one had invented in-car speakers. Loudspeakers supplied the sound to the drive-in's patrons and often beyond, to its annoyed neighbors. An equally serious problem was that distributors weren't eager to rent films for it. Decades later, Hollingshead told the *Philadelphia Inquirer* that one of his first rentals "was three years old and cost us $400 for four days. The last time the film had run was in a little (theater) that paid $20 a week for it." He sold that Camden drive-in theater within three years to an indoor theater owner (with better film connections) who moved it to Union NJ.

The Hollingshead patent didn't fare much better, as most competitors built similar sites without paying royalties. But potential drive-in builders weren't sure they could safely ignore the patent. That uncertainty, along with the early sound problems, kept the drive-in business from growing quickly. Fewer than two dozen permanent drive-in theaters were built in the first five years, often using naming alternatives such as "motor-in" or "outdoor theatre." Some small-town entrepreneurs

An early advancement in sound came in 1940 in Providence RI. That city's drive-in added in-car amplifiers, which were attached each night by attendants. The installation for 550 cars cost $10,000, or about $200,000 in today's dollars. In this photo from *The Exhibitor*, manager Walter D. McGhee shows off one of the eight-inch devices.

operated short-lived versions using little more than bedsheets, loudspeakers, and film projectors. When the *Film Daily Year Book* published the first national drive-in theater list in 1942, it could find only 95 of them.

The Postwar Explosion

World War II ended, and American soldiers returned home ready to start families and enjoy some entertainment. For most, their choices were live performance, radio, or the movies. Television was only available in some of the big cities, and it was really expensive. A typical 1951 set cost over $2500 in today's dollars and could receive just three black and white broadcasts on a screen smaller than today's computer monitors. The only way to watch a movie was to see whatever was showing, a current film or a reissue, at a theater.

One factor that accelerated the drive-in boom was the postwar availability of the inexpensive in-car speaker. Its classic shape symbolized the drive-in age. 2019 photo by the author at the National Route 66 Museum in Elk City OK.

    So in the early postwar years, every factor lined up in favor of drive-ins. The rapidly growing population increasingly moved to suburbs and away from traditional downtown theaters. For those indoor theaters, parking could be difficult or expensive, patrons were expected to dress up, and families with children needed to find babysitters.

    Outdoor movies had none of those drawbacks. Patrons were urged to "come as you are" and bring the kids along. Daylight time wasn't widespread yet, so drive-ins could start at a decent hour. Hollywood slowly switched to movies in color, even as it continued to create films suitable for the whole family. Plentiful cheap land at the edge of town beckoned developers. As car ownership rapidly became ubiquitous, families had a fun new place to go.

A Brief History of Drive-Ins

Drive-in theaters built increasingly elaborate playgrounds, which drew children, who brought their parents along. They were often monitored by attendants, such as the clown shown above at Long Island NY's Bayshore-Sunrise Drive-In, which also had a motor-driven Ferris wheel. Photo from the 1955-56 *Theatre Catalog*.

The number of drive-ins grew steadily, but the real explosion came after October 1949 when the US Supreme Court ruled, in effect, that Hollingshead's ramp could not be patented. In one year, the number of US drive-ins more than doubled, from about 750 in 1949 to over 1700 in 1950. That number would have grown even higher, but in September 1950, as the Korean War flared, the US National Production Authority began requiring its approval to use certain building materials for entertainment facilities. Despite that speed bump, drive-in construction resumed normally within a couple of years, and the drive-in population grew to over 4300 by 1955. After that high point, the number leveled out for the next decade.

The Long Decline

After the drive-in population plateaued, most of the factors that led to their growth peeled away one by one. Television expanded to almost every city, and TV set prices dropped from unthinkable to merely expensive. Families snapped them up; 83 percent of American homes had TV in 1958, up from a mere 9 percent in 1950.

At all theaters, fewer films worked for the whole family; most explored more mature topics, and some were too childish for grown-ups to enjoy. Casual wear became acceptable at indoor theaters, and there were more of them close to home near suburban shopping centers. National adoption of Daylight Saving Time in 1967 sliced a crucial hour off already limited drive-in schedules.

Possibly the greatest single factor in the death of so many drive-ins was the arrival of the video cassette recorder (VCR). Few drive-ins survived the 1980s, the decade when VCRs became common in homes. Photo © olegkrugllyak | Depositphotos.com.

A Brief History of Drive-Ins

Movie-viewing at home became more convenient. Home Box Office launched in 1972, the first of a wave of commercial-free, uncut movie channels for home viewing. Perhaps the final, most lethal drive-in killer was the video cassette recorder. As VCRs dropped in price, video rental stores popped up. A family could line up a double- or triple-feature with homemade snacks for less than the cost of a night out.

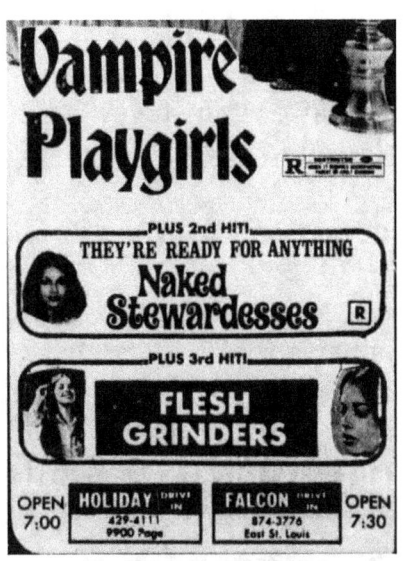

Part of a 1980 *St. Louis Post-Dispatch* ad for a triple feature of racy movies at two nearby drive-ins, both included in this book.

Many drive-ins reacted by trying to provide viewers with an experience they couldn't get on television. In the mid-1950s, that meant wide-screen movies, and most pre-existing drive-ins added wings to their screens. Westerns and other family fare faded. As the typical car became less likely to include children, drive-in movie-makers shifted their attention to teenagers and young adults. In the 1960s and 1970s, that often meant horror or titillation films, which were eventually labeled as R-rated. Some drive-ins went even further, showing softcore sexy R movies or even hardcore adult films.

As cities and suburbs expanded, they often encircled previously remote drive-ins. When a developer wanted a contiguous piece of land for a shopping mall or a housing tract, he could offer to buy a drive-in. Some landowners had figured this out decades earlier, offering short-term leases to drive-in theaters while planning to cash out once their parcels became valuable. Combine that with the dwindling crowds and neighborhood pressure against X-rated movies, selling out was often the landowner's best choice.

21st Century Rediscovery

Most drive-ins that persisted past the year 2000 were either popular in small but not tiny towns (about 5,000-10,000 people), or were in metropolitan areas stuck on parcels of land that were unappealing for other uses. For the survivors, a few new factors tilted back their way.

When most cars included FM radios, that allowed drive-in operators to switch to less expensive FM radio sound. Photo of a 1982 AMC station wagon by Christopher Ziemnowicz.

A Brief History of Drive-Ins 11

Disney had always produced family-friendly movies, and it kick-started a modern-day trend with Best Picture nominee *Beauty and the Beast* (1991). Hoping for similar success, other filmmakers returned to making animated movies that the whole family could enjoy. Studios expanded production of comic book adaptations and other cartoonish action movies, so drive-ins once again had a product to sell to both children and their parents. The FM radio transmitter supplemented and often replaced window-hanging speakers since most cars now had FM stereo radios. Patrons enjoyed richer movie audio than they had from a single, tinny speaker, and drive-in owners didn't have to maintain and replace speakers every month.

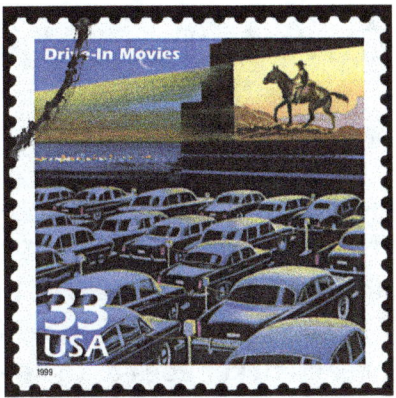

The USPS issued a drive-in theater stamp in 1999 as part of its "Celebrate the Century" set. It was one of 16 representing the 1950s. Photo © Mmphotos2017 | Dreamstime.com

Near the close of the last century, when the US Postal Service asked its users to vote on the topic that best commemorated the 1950s, they were surprised that the big winner was drive-in movies. Postwar baby boomer children had become parents themselves and grew nostalgic for the advantages and fun of the drive-in. Surviving drive-ins showed an uptick in attendance around the turn of the century.

But that didn't mean they were out of the woods. Almost no new drive-ins were being built, and every year, a few drive-ins closed as their aging owner-managers cashed out, retired, or both.

Drive-In Economics

Let me pause for a moment to describe a typical drive-in theater's sources of income. In the early days, drive-ins often rented or even purchased films and kept the ticket proceeds. In 1954, concession stand sales accounted for just 22% of the average drive-in's income. Those days are long gone. Today, a very high percentage of each ticket goes to the movie's distributor, so modern drive-ins make most of their money through the concession stand.

In effect, most drive-in theaters operate as seasonal outdoor restaurants with an entertainment theme. They're popular and a lot more fun, but keeping that in mind, you can see how it's hard to get rich by running a drive-in. It also explains why some drive-in owners get really cheesed when patrons bring in their own food. The best drive-ins sell food so good that you'd look forward to choosing it for dinner. Even for the bad ones, I still make a point to buy popcorn and soda, a drive-in's most profitable products. But I have digressed long enough. Back to history.

The Digital Imperative

Theatrical digital movie projection, using hard drives instead of reels of film, was first demonstrated in 1999. After 15 years of tweaking the format and planning a new distribution system, Hollywood decided to switch. The word came down from studios that they would no longer spend $5 million or more per movie to print a limited number of copies on fragile, heavy film. They required all theaters to convert to digital projection so they could use easier-to-ship, reusable hard drives instead.

A Brief History of Drive-Ins

If buying a single drive-in digital projector is expensive, imagine laying out the cash for nine of them. Here are three of the Glendale (AZ) 9 Drive-In's digital projectors. 2013 photo by the author.

Drive-ins always needed powerful film projectors to show films. Their larger screens sat farther away than indoor theaters', and ambient city light interfered more than a darkened room. To comply with Hollywood's demand, they needed special, expensive digital projectors. As I just mentioned, drive-ins typically don't clear a ton of money, so many of them feared that they'd have to close when the last film versions of movies disappeared.

In 2013, Honda spotlighted these owners' plight through Project Drive-In, where fans could vote for their favorite theater. Honda awarded projectors to nine winners, and the contest drew public attention to the drive-ins that didn't win.

When the final wave of digital conversion hit soon after, some drive-ins shut down, but not as many as some had feared. And here's the thing — those that survived found that whatever hadn't killed them made them stronger.

The digital system has its benefits. Picture quality is always excellent. "Prints" of any movie are more easily available. Drive-in screens can show broadcast sports or huge video games. And having invested all that money in equipment, today's drive-ins have a stronger incentive to stay open year after year. Brand-new drive-ins are being built, and new-wave "pop-up" boutique drive-ins thrive in converted parking lots. During the Covid pandemic, more people came to appreciate the natural social distancing and excellent ventilation that drive-ins offer.

The steady pressure of rising land value continues to close a few drive-ins every year. But some of the original attractions of a drive-in are now causing about as many to pop up in their place. Substitute FM radio sound for a loudspeaker and once again, all a theatrical entrepreneur really needs is a projector, a screen, and a parking lot.

The Blue Starlite Mini Urban (sic) Drive-In Theater in Minturn CO is a great example of the new style of pop-up drive-in. 2017 photo by the author.

A Brief History of Route 66

The history of US Highway 66 is a lot like the history of drive-in theaters. The Mother Road started slow, when few people used it, picked up a lot of momentum after World War II, had a few decades of overwhelming popularity, faded in the 1980s, and experienced a nostalgia-fueled resurgence over the past 20 years or so. But John Steinbeck never wrote about drive-in theaters.

Dividing Up the Highway Numbers

Roads between cities were a piecemeal affair a century ago. Some organizations tried to rally local governments to pave the roads between cities, creating named roads such as the Yellowstone Trail, the Lincoln Highway, and the Ozark Trails. That last set of roads went from St. Louis to Santa Rosa NM via Joplin, Tulsa, Oklahoma City, and Amarillo.

In 1925, the American Association of State Highway and Transportation Officials set up the Joint Board on Interstate Highways to establish an easier system of numbered routes. As part of the general plan they hashed out, major north-south highway numbers would end in a 1 or 5, and major east-west highways would end in 0. Route 60 would go from Chicago to Los Angeles via Tulsa, as desired by Cyrus Avery, local promoter and former chairman of the Oklahoma Highway Commission. Officials from Kentucky objected, wanting a 0-number highway of their own. They lobbied hard enough to pull 60 away, leaving 62 for the road that used

Tulsa honored the Father of Route 66 with the Cyrus Avery Centennial Plaza. Photo © 4kclips | Depositphotos.com

so much of the Ozark Trails. Avery's group didn't like 62 and soon settled for 66, a catchier number.

Avery helped form the US Highway 66 Association in 1927. Delegates from eight states met in Tulsa (of course) to plan paving and promote Route 66 as "the Main Street of America."

The Road Grows and Evolves

The first priority for Route 66 was to pave it. That wasn't a problem for Illinois, which already had the paved state highway 4 between Chicago and St. Louis, so it just changed signs. It wasn't a problem for Kansas, which had earlier paved its 13 or so miles. Other states had a lower priority for the work. Oklahoma didn't finish paving its (admittedly longer) section of 66 until 1937. Texas' highway department concentrated its efforts to

Most segments of Route 66 were two-lane highways, with plenty of driveways and distractions along the way. 1955 photo by the Missouri Department of Transportation from the Missouri State Archives.

benefit its larger cities, all well south of the panhandle, so it didn't complete its much smaller chunk until 1938.

The next priority for Route 66 was to get travelers to use it. The US Highway 66 Association took out an ad in *The Saturday Evening Post* in 1932, promoting "the Great Diagonal Highway" to the Olympics in Los Angeles. Then a whole wave of travelers, more like refugees, took to 66 beginning in 1934, when the Dust Bowl's windblown soil erosion forced tens of thousands of poverty-stricken families to abandon their farms and migrate to California. Their plight was captured in John Steinbeck's 1939 novel *The Grapes of Wrath*, the book which christened the migrant highway "The Mother Road."

Partly because of its early birth, Route 66 changed its course like a river, shifting to new configurations between major cities as needed. Highway engineers kept learning from their mistakes and making better roads to handle interstate traffic. In Illinois, for example, a new 66 highway, designed for faster speed from Chicago to St. Louis, opened in 1940, skipping the towns of Thayer and Carlinville in favor of Litchfield and Farmersville.

Postwar Boom Times

In 1946, Nat King Cole recorded Bobby Troup's song, "(Get Your Kicks On) Route 66," giving the highway with a catchy number a catchy tune to go with it. Drivers responded. The increased traffic the 66 association had always wanted now added pressure for more lanes.

Beginning in the 1940s, many sections were widened to four lanes, and some bypassed towns instead of crawling through their bustling downtown areas. The newly neglected businesses wanted to keep some kind of highway, which led to an array of alternates. The list included City 66, Spur 66, Bypass 66, Optional 66, Alternate 66, Business 66, and my favorite, Alternate Business 66, a second business route in Springfield MO.

Will Rogers, the beloved homespun humorist who died in a plane crash in 1935, got the Hollywood biopic treatment in 1952, and the US Highway 66 Association

The Painted Desert, part of the Petrified Forest National Park in Arizona, was another natural wonder to delight Route 66 travelers. 2018 photo from the Carol M. Highsmith Archive, Library of Congress, Prints and Photographs Division.

designated US 66 as the Will Rogers Highway. It wasn't official, but the association added historical markers all along the route.

By the 1950s, nearly every US family finally owned a car, and motorists chose Route 66 for their vacations, especially for long road trips to and from southern California. The highway passed several natural tourist destinations, such as Arizona's meteor crater, Petrified Forest, and Grand Canyon. Entrepreneurs added less natural tourist draws such as reptile farms, Indian trinket workshops, and teepee-shaped motels. Tourist caves, such as Meramec Caverns and Grand Canyon Caverns, blurred the line between natural wonders and artificial lures.

Fast food grew up along 66. Springfield MO had Red's Giant Hamburg, believed to be the first drive-through restaurant. Springfield IL still has the Cozy Drive-In, which served up some of the earliest corn dogs, called Cozy Dogs there. And the first McDonald's was born on the Mother Road in San Bernardino CA.

In 1960-64, CBS aired the TV series *Route 66* featuring two photogenic, footloose young men driving around the country and getting involved in local dramas. Despite its name, the show's weekly locations

This Route 66 icon came about after owner Sheldon "Red" Chaney gave his signmakers incorrect measurements. 2020 photo from the Carol M. Highsmith Archive, Library of Congress, Prints and Photographs Division.

rarely included US 66. The series provided another boost to the highway, but the Mother Road's demise had already been guaranteed.

The Long Decline

During World War II, General Dwight Eisenhower saw the efficiency of Germany's divided autobahn highways. As president, he signed the Interstate Highway Act of 1956, providing federal funds for a similar system. In 1962, the US Highway 66 Association asked the feds to name the Chicago to Los Angeles route Interstate 66, but the feds shook their heads and said, in effect, "That's not how this works." Each section of the new road was given a different number: I-10, I-15, I-40, I-44, and I-55.

The Chain of Rocks Bridge closed to cars in 1970. Years later it was refurbished as a pedestrian/cycling bridge with Route 66 souvenirs. 2009 photo from Carol M. Highsmith's America, Library of Congress, Prints and Photographs Division.

A Brief History of Route 66

Even more than the widened stretches of US 66, the new interstate highways bypassed small towns and tourist facilities. Making matters worse, the Highway Beautification Act of 1965 limited the number of billboards along those interstates, so it was difficult for bypassed businesses to attract drivers from the new roads.

Motorists loved the new interstates, which were, and still are, better in a lot of ways. They're faster, more efficient, and much safer than the old roads they replaced. In 1985, weeks after the last segment of I-40 was completed near Williams AZ, US 66 was officially decommissioned.

Neglect, Then Nostalgia

Cut off from federal highway money, most remaining sections of the old Route 66 decayed. When David Knudson decided in 1994 to retrace his route from Chicago to Los Angeles 30 years earlier, he couldn't find it. The Mother Road wasn't on any maps or road signs.

This Seligman AZ icon, Delgadillo's Snow Cap drive-in, seems to be as popular today as it ever was. 2016 photo from the Carol M. Highsmith Archive, Library of Congress, Prints and Photographs Division.

So he and his wife Mary Lou founded the National Historic Route 66 Federation to inform the public about this long ribbon of cultural heritage. In 1999, with the Federation's backing, Congress passed the National Route 66 Preservation Bill, providing federal matching funds to anyone working to preserve or restore historic properties along the road. Route 66 signs returned, and now it's not too difficult to follow the old highway along its remaining segments.

The 2006 Pixar movie *Cars*, set in fictional Radiator Springs on the very real Route 66, added to the growing Mother Road nostalgia. And how did that movie end? With the characters watching *Toy Car Story*, *Monster Trucks Inc.*, and *A Bug's Life* — a rare triple feature — at the freshly restored Radiator Springs Drive-In Theatre. Welcome to the Drive-Ins of Route 66.

If you search online for "Radiator Springs Drive-In Theater," you can find a perfect screen capture from the closing credits of the movie *Cars*. There's a full-sized mural on the screen tower, its name is outlined in neon, and the restored sign in the foreground dazzles with four colors of neon. I can't afford the license to show you that, so I'll make do with this real-life photo of Flo's V8 Cafe in Cars Land at Disney California Adventure Park. © Lucy Clark | Dreamstime.com.

Illinois

Although Route 66 began (or ended) in Chicago, only about seven miles of it ran through the city's southwest side. Although there were quite a few drive-ins in the suburbs, the only ozoner within Chicago's city limits was the Double (1950-1995).

Cicero

Cicero is the first municipality on the Mother Road after leaving Chicago. This suburb, most famous for being the former home of Al Capone, is the 11th most populous town in the state. Cicero's only drive-in was a literal stone's throw from the Chicago city limits.

Bel-Air Drive-In

Opened: March 2, 1956

Closed: Sept. 17, 2000

Capacity: 2300 cars

Location: About a half-mile south of Route 66 on Cicero Avenue.

The abandoned quarry that would become the Bel-Air was being used as a dumping ground just before construction began in 1955. Cicero town officials were happy to see the smelly eyesore replaced by a modern drive-in. Its builders, Belmont Amusement Corp. leveled the garbage and other materials, then covered it with a couple of feet of clay and a few layers of gravel. It opened

The Bel-Air's two-sided screen was the first to go up, in 1956. Management built the third screen in 1979. Photo, circa 2000, by DarkstarMike via CinemaTreasures.org.

the next spring after a warm day had melted the leftover snow on the ground. That evening, many of the cars sank to their axles in the soft clay and required tractors to pull them out. The drive-in took a break for a few days while the ground hardened.

The Bel-Air was a huge drive-in, advertised as the world's largest. Its double-sided screen, also advertised as the world's largest, pointed at two lots which together held more than 2000 cars. The drive-in was run by M & R Theaters, the company founded by Martin and Richard Rosenfeld and Raymond Marks, which also ran the Double Drive-In and other Chicago-area theaters. They would add a third screen in June 1979.

By the late 1960s, the garbage under the drive-in started causing problems. The Cicero Anti-Blight Department told the Bel-Air to stop burning trash, clean up piles of broken concrete, and do something about the rodent infestation. The drive-in's management addressed the problems to the satisfaction of the city,

The Bel-Air opened with a double feature on just one side of its double screen, as shown in its ad in the *Chicago Tribune*.

though anecdotes suggest that the viewing fields were far from pristine.

In October 1977, an off-duty Cicero policeman saw *Cinderella* advertised on the Bel-Air marquee, so he drove his family over to watch. Unfortunately, the movie was the softcore adult film *Cinderella 2000*, which led to the family's quick retreat, followed by a cease and desist order from the city. After promising to cut the film down to an R rating, management was allowed to continue showing the movie, but only on the south screen, where it couldn't be seen by teenagers from the 1st Street Bridge.

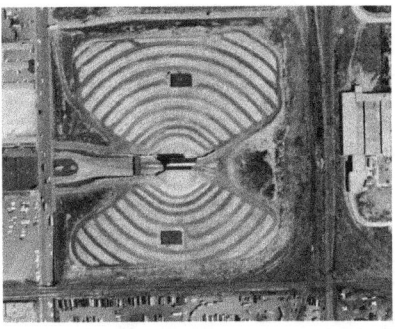

The north viewing field was the Bel-Air's largest, as shown in this 1962 photo, taken before the third screen was built. © HistoricAerials.com, used by permission.

The Cicero Health Department closed the Bel-Air before the start of the 1996 season amid allegations that the land under the clay and gravel included illegally received toxic "automobile fluff." That pit may have been one of the targets of the FBI's "Operation Silver Shovel" investigation of public corruption relating to Chicago-area dumps. The drive-in stayed closed all year, then as it ramped up to open in 1997, the health department closed it again. In response, Loews Chicago Cinema sued the city, claiming that the continuing shutdown was a result of their failure to contribute to the Town Republican Organization golf outing. Somehow, that all got cleared up, and the Bel-Air reopened in August 1997.

The drive-in closed three years later, after the 2000 season. Tangled in a web of Environmental Protection Agency cleanups, and with Cicero considering eminent domain proceedings, the lot remains vacant today.

Countryside

This small suburb didn't incorporate until 1960, long after Route 66 and the 66 Drive-In had been built. Except perhaps for the Theodore State Forest, the most prominent feature within its borders is the Countryside Plaza Shopping Center on the site of the former drive-in.

66 Drive-In

Opened: May 28, 1948

Closed: Sept. 12, 1976

Capacity: 900 cars

Location: A few hundred feet north of Route 66 on La Grange Road. When it was built, the drive-in was in unincorporated land just south of La Grange and east of Lyons; contemporary accounts listed the 66 Drive-In under one of those cities.

The Phillip Smith Company from Boston reportedly spent over $250,000 to build the 66, which it opened in the spring of 1948. From the start, the drive-in's trademark was its aggressive hustling for customers. Its

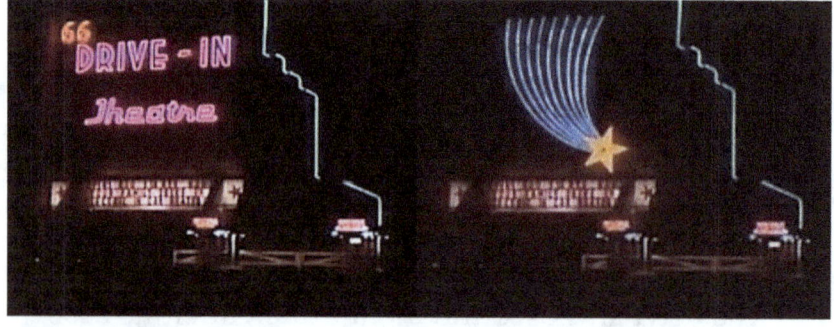

The impressive neon display on the 66's screen tower blinked a colorful falling star. Assembled from two photos posted by salc65 on CinemaTreasures.org.

children's playground was supplemented by free pony rides. Its scramble for first-run films and the beginnings of a ticket price war soon led to a truce among Chicago-area drive-in operators in April 1951. They all agreed on 80 cents as the price for adults, and promised not to run carload specials.

That anti-competitive truce drove the 66 to find other ways to gain an edge. That summer, manager Ken Prickett used radio broadcasts from the 66 to advertise his drive-in. In 1952, he teamed with Road King gas stations to offer a free gallon to anyone who bought his popcorn. That was also the year the 66 tried out "guest car" nights, where all autos of a particular make were admitted free.

In 1954, the 66 widened its screen. In October, it presented a dusk-to-dawn promotion of seven films for a single ticket (now 85 cents). Anyone who stayed to the end got free coffee and donuts from concession manager Norman Bates. In-car heaters arrived in 1956, and Smith's company changed its name to General Drive-In (in 1960) then General Cinema (1964).

Western Outdoor Management bought the 66 in early 1976 and would run it for only one season. Just weeks after its final double feature, developers tore down the drive-in to make way for the shopping center that still occupies the site today.

Romeoville

Romeo and Juliet were the names of two of the towns laid out in the early 19th century by the commissioners of the Illinois and Michigan Shipping Canal. In 1845, Juliet's city fathers changed that name to honor explorer Louis Jolliet. In 1895, when Romeo's residents incorporated their village, they changed its name to Romeoville.

Bel-Air Drive-In

Opened: July 1949

Closed: 1987?

Capacity: 1000 cars

Location: On Alt-66, now Independence Blvd, south of its intersection with 135th Street/Romeo Road.

Thomas I. Wagner was a big promoter of Joliet. He was a former president of the rotary club and of the chamber of commerce there. In the fall of 1948, he organized a group of local businessmen to form the Bel Air Theatre Company, with an eye on building a large drive-in just outside the city limits, in what is now Romeoville.

The next spring, the Lotz Sign Company built the 12-foot high letters on the back of the Bel-Air's screen tower. In all, the sign took 12,000 feet of neon tubing, weighed 3½ tons, and was called "the largest sign ever to be displayed in Will County." The drive-in was originally scheduled to open on June 1, but the actual opener slid to late July or early August 1949.

The Bel-Air's ownership history is a little fuzzy. Wagner managed the place, and either he or his corporation were mentioned as owners at first. The 1952 *Theatre Catalog* said that the owner was the H. and E. (Harry and Elmer) Balaban Circuit, then the 1955-56 edition said that it was co-owned by Balaban and Bel Air Theatres.

The Feb. 6, 1952 issue of *Boxoffice* noted that during the off-season, the Bel-Air's manager rented the drive-in's marquee to advertise an auto dealer.

By early 1965, another theater chain, L&M Management, owned the Bel-Air. By 1983, L&M was selling off its theaters, especially its drive-ins. General manager George Collins told the *Rockford Register Star* that bad weather had hurt their thin profits. "There've been three terrible springs in a row," he said. Exactly when L&M closed the Bel-Air is also uncertain. A 1988 aerial photo showed the site completely razed, so it had to have been by 1987. Storage units occupy the site today.

Joliet

Joliet is the third-most populous city in Illinois. Among movie fans, it's most notable for the Joliet Correctional Center, which closed in 2002 but was featured in *The Blues Brothers* and the TV series *Prison Break*. The Joliet Area Historical Museum offers tours of the prison.

Hilltop Drive-In

Opened: August 1949

Closed: 2001

Capacity: 500 cars

Location: On US 6 about 2½ miles east of Alt-66 as it passed through Joliet.

Spelling note: Although its screen tower and grand opening ad included a hyphen in "Hill-Top," most subsequent references and advertisements omitted it.

This drive-in went through a lot of owners. First, Rube Levine built the Hilltop in 1949. In early 1951, Harry and Elmer Balaban bought it. The next ownership group, who held it for about five years, was the most flamboyant.

The Hilltop's concrete-block tower, unchanged since 1949, stood strong well into the 21st Century before a tornado took it down in 2020. © Robert Philip | Dreamstime.com

In his book, *A Youth in Babylon,* David Friedman wrote about using some of the proceeds that he and Irwin Joseph had amassed showing the once-scandalous film *Mom and Dad* as a down payment to buy the Hilltop from the Balabans in 1959. Friedman and Joseph owned Modern Film Distributors, creator of several racy exploitation films. One such movie, *The Adventures of Lucky Pierre,* was reportedly filmed at the Hilltop, but Joseph never showed any of his movies there, calling it a "high-class drive-in." Joseph bought out Friedman's share of the Hilltop in 1963. Soon after, he added tons of sand in front of the screen and held a faux beach party while showing the movie *Beach Party.*

Joseph passed away in the summer of 1964, and his widow kept the Hilltop for another year before passing it along to the Joliet View Corp., headed by former Chicago-area RKO Theatres manager Jerry Shimbach.

Early in 1967, the owners of the nearby Bel-Air Drive-In, L&M Theatres, bought the Hilltop. Among its many owners, L&M kept the Hilltop alive the longest, until about 1986.

In 1995, three guys, Saul Ornelas and Adrian and Arturo Contreras, reopened the Hilltop for a few years. A note at CinemaTreasures.org suggested that they leased it "to an acquaintance who mismanaged it badly," and the drive-in closed after the 2001 season.

The owners converted some of the back ramps to soccer fields, and the site stayed active. The Hilltop's sturdy screen tower remained, spurring speculation about reopening the drive-in one day, until a tornado toppled it in August 2020.

Pontiac

Pontiac hosts the Route 66 Association of Illinois Hall of Fame and Museum. The Pontiac Museum Complex also includes the Walldog Mural Exhibit, commemorating the artists who designed and painted advertisements on the sides of brick buildings.

Pontiac / Star Chief Drive-In

Opened: July 1949

Closed: September 6, 1981

Capacity: 275 cars

Location: On Custer Avenue on Pontiac's northwest side, just a few feet west of Route 66.

K. Gordon Murray was a pioneer in exploitation filmmaking and promotion. His Mexican import *Santa Claus*, which he narrated, was hugely profitable in children's matinees. Some of his earlier work had earned a "Condemned" rating from the National Legion of Decency. Before all that, the Bloomington IL native partnered with his father to build the Pontiac Drive-In in the summer of 1949.

Ken Murray owned the Pontiac for only a year before leaving for Hollywood to work for Cecil B. DeMille. Thomas E. Lally became the new owner, and he ran the drive-in until suffering a stroke in the fall of 1953. School superintendent Leonard Hewitt was the next to run the Pontiac. Kenneth Phillips, one of the men who built the Phil-Kron in Bloomington, soon bought the Pontiac and renamed it the Star Chief, sometimes written hyphenated or as one word.

Before the 1958 season, Phillips sold the Star Chief

When the Kerasotes chain reopened the Star Chief for the first time in 1958, it started the season with a free movie, advertising it in the Bloomington *Pantagraph*.

and the Phil-Kron to the Kerasotes Theatres chain of Springfield. That was the year that the drive-in showed Murray's most notorious, condemned double-feature, *Wasted Lives* and *The Birth of Twins*. The Star Chief's following decades marked a period of quiet corporate operation. It closed for the 1981 season on Labor Day weekend; the following May, Kerasotes announced that it would not reopen the Star Chief, citing "low attendance." Small offices and large truck parking occupy the site today.

Bloomington

Two big draws to Bloomington are Route 66 and Abraham Lincoln lore, so the McLean County Museum of History combined them in a visitor center exhibit called "Cruisin' with Lincoln on 66." Its logo shows a silhouette of our 16th president behind the wheel of a convertible, wearing his stovepipe hat.

Phil-Kron / Bloomington Drive-In

Opened: July 3, 1947

Closed: 1984

Capacity: 850 cars and 400 seats

Location: Immediately north of Route 66 on Main Street.

Ken Phillips was the long-time owner of a painting company in Bloomington in 1947 when he partnered with Greek immigrant Peter Karonis to build a combination drive-in and grill, advertised as "The Only One of Its Kind in the World." The Phil-Kron's screen was 37x42 feet.

The partners had to repair the projection booth after a gas explosion in the 1952 offseason blew out two of its walls. In 1953, Phillips and Karonis said they would build another drive-in north of town. That fell through. In 1957, they added a mini-golf course, an amusement park, and an expanded snack bar.

The metal screen that Kerasotes erected to replace the original Phil-Kron tower, blown down in 1963, was as featureless as the name "Drive-In." But Peter Karonis' Sinorak restaurant endured. 1980 photo, John Margolies Roadside America photograph archive (1972-2008), Library of Congress, Prints and Photographs Division.

The Kerasotes Theatres chain arrived in 1958 before the season started, buying the Phil-Kron and Pontiac's Star Chief, also owned by Phillips. Kerasotes announced that Bloomington's drive-in would be known as Drive-In Theatre. The restaurant, not part of the sale, changed its name to the Sinorak, the owner's name backwards.

In 1963, a storm leveled the screen and the restaurant, but both were rebuilt. The Sinorak closed in 1980, then was destroyed in a September 1984 fire that damaged the screen. R. T. Dunn Drive now runs through the old viewing field, mostly occupied by storage units.

Lincoln

Lincoln IL is the only US city that was named for Abraham Lincoln before he became president. In 1853, he was working for the Chicago & Mississippi Railroad and assisted in selling the city's first pieces of land. The story goes that when folks proposed the name, he said, "Nothing bearing the name of Lincoln ever amounted to much."

Bennis Auto Vue Drive-In

Opened: September? 1950

Closed: Aug. 29, 1982

Capacity: 400 cars

Location: On Route 66 at the northeast corner of Lincoln.

One of Greek immigrant Steve Bennis's first jobs was at a candy concession at the St. Louis World's Fair in 1904. Later that year, he moved to Lincoln and opened his own candy kitchen and store. Bennis later managed an indoor theater in Lincoln, then opened his own open-air Airdome theater near downtown. In 1915, he sold the Airdome and opened a theater in the back of his candy shop. Patrons had to walk through the store to get to the 200-seat theater, and I'll bet some of them bought some snacks for the movie. At a time when concessions were an afterthought for theater managers, this made Bennis something of a pioneer.

In 1923, Bennis built the 1,000-seat Lincoln Theater, then closed the candy-shop theater. He soon bought one local competitor, the Grand, and in 1949 finally bought Lincoln's other indoor theater, the Vogue.

In September 1949, just a few months after buying the Vogue, Bennis announced that he would build the city's first drive-in. Despite that planning, and despite an earlier start to construction, Bennis's drive-in opened after the Lincoln Drive-In. But the Auto Vue would last much longer than its southside rival.

The Bennis Auto Vue's life was quiet. Bennis himself passed away in 1954 at the age of 72. His movie business, which included five indoor theaters and two drive-ins, kept rolling along. The Auto Vue closed for the season the weekend before Labor Day 1982 and didn't reopen. Nothing remains of the drive-in today.

One secret for drive-in longevity is finding an odd parcel of land. In the Auto Vue's case, it was a narrow corner bounded by US 66 to the north and the Illinois Central Railroad to the southeast. Detail of a 1973 USGS aerial photo.

Lincoln Drive-In

Opened: August? 1950

Closed: October 1953

Capacity: 475 cars

Location: Just over two miles from Route 66 at the southeast edge of Lincoln at what was then Broadway and Route 121. They've reworked the intersections since then; now the site is a field across County Road 1500 from Chester-East Lincoln School.

Four men from Terre Haute IN, W. H. McKee, Al Byrd, and F. B. Youngblood and his son William, moved in on Steve Bennis's territory, building the Lincoln Drive-In over the summer of 1950. They opened the Lincoln before Bennis's Auto Vue was completed.

Its proximity to a creek on its south side left the flat drive-in subject to flooding, leading some residents to nickname it the "Lincoln Dive-In." William Youngblood moved to town and got married in 1951. He lived in a trailer on the drive-in's grounds, and the Lincoln's 3½ seasons passed uneventfully.

The quiet times came to a shattering end on March 12, 1954. A massive windstorm demolished the screen, scattered pieces of the fence up to five miles away, and rolled Youngblood's trailer nearly 100 feet. Fortunately there were no reported injuries, but the partnership never rebuilt. They sold the drive-in to the Bennis family a month later, and the ground sat idle for years. Although it's still just a grassy field, even the ramps are completely gone today.

An ad in the *Lincoln Evening Courier*, via Finding Lincoln Illinois.

Springfield

There are several confusing stories of renamed drive-ins along Route 66, and Springfield is where we find the first of them. The Illinois capitol was home to a 66 Drive-In, which was a huge, frequently photographed icon on the Mother Road. That drive-in is long gone. Decades later, the owners of the former Green Meadows renamed it the Route 66 Drive-In.

Springfield Drive-In

Opened: Sept. 19, 1947

Closed: Oct. 2, 1983

Capacity: 1200 cars and 100 seats

Location: East of town on Dirksen Parkway, just east of Route 66.

Waukegan attorney Joseph Sikes broke ground just outside the Springfield city limits in the summer of 1947. George Peterson was the architect of what was then called simply "Drive-In Theatre." Despite construction delays from bad weather, Sikes managed to get it open before the end of the season that year. The screen tower was 75 feet high and 84 feet wide, holding a 62-foot wide screen. The concession-projection building was made of concrete blocks painted white.

Sikes made a few improvements during the following offseason. He increased the capacity from 800 cars to 900. The rest rooms became "fully equipped," which makes me worry what they were like the year before. Sikes also added a playground in 1948. At the end of that first full season, he partnered with Ralph Lawler, who owned the Peoria Drive-In. By the start of the 1950 season, the drive-in had grown to hold 1100 cars.

When the Springfield Drive-In opened, it was pretty much in the middle of nowhere. By the time it closed, it was surrounded by other businesses. Photo from the Sangamon Valley Collection at Lincoln Library, Springfield IL.

At the close of the 1952 season, the Frisina Amusement Company of Springfield bought the drive-in from Sikes. Frisina expanded the concession building and added a miniature train and a merry-go-round. In the 1960s, Frisina added a second, larger concession building behind the first.

There followed a couple of decades of quiet corporate ownership. The Springfield Drive-In began showing racier movies by the late 1970s. Illinois had passed a law in 1974 prohibiting outdoor movie screens from distracting motorists. The Springfield's screen predated that law, so drivers on I-55 got an eyeful.

By 1980, enough of the Springfield's movies were explicit enough to cause the city to react. On March 7, 1981, the state's attorney's office raided the drive-in while it was showing the adult film *Seduction*. The following month, a Frisina officer pleaded guilty on behalf of the corporation to a misdemeanor charge of distributing harmful material. The drive-in was fined $300 and agreed to stay away from hardcore films. For the rest of 1981, the Springfield showed a mixture of general-release films and hard-R drive-in movies.

Mid America Theaters, based in Sharon Springs KS, bought the Springfield along with 25 other Frisina theaters in October 1981. The new owner pledged to continue avoiding explicit movies, and that's how it went until the drive-in closed after the 1983 season.

Flea markets continued on the Springfield Drive-In site for a few years, and a nearby Buick dealership used the screen tower for ads. In the spring of 1991, a wind storm damaged the old screen, and it was soon dismantled. Today, a trucking company occupies the site, which still contains Frisina's second concession building.

Bonus: (Kerasotes) Twin Drive-In

Opened: May 10, 1973

Closed: Sept. 6, 1984

Capacity: 1400 cars

Location: On the southwest side of town between US 36 and Wabash Avenue, about two miles west of Route 66's original alignment. By the time the drive-in was built, it was about 4.2 miles from Route 66, so it really doesn't qualify for this list. I mistakenly included it in the first edition of this book, so here it is again.

The Kerasotes Theaters chain announced in January 1968 that it was going to build a twin-screen drive-in next to US 36 on the west side of town. They finally got around to construction in April 1972, and pretty much finished construction by October that year, waiting until the following spring to open.

(By the way, I'm unsure of the right name for this drive-in. Its sign had "Twin Drive-In" in large letters and a tiny "Kerasotes" above it. Its grand opening ad had "Twin" in huge letters with a tiny "Kerasotes" inside the "T". Contemporary newspaper stories called it simply the "Twin," but some folks think that its correct name was "Kerasotes Twin." I'll use the shorter name.)

This detail of a Kerasotes ad in the Jan. 14, 1973 *Daily Illinois State Journal* showed the drive-in's sign. The text above it suggested its name was the Twin.

The Twin included two 40x100-foot steel screens with a projection/concession booth in the middle. Each of the two lots held about 700 cars. But the modern drive-in lasted only 12 seasons before it became another victim of changing movie habits. Kerasotes used the building as a warehouse for a few years, and they leveled some of the ramps to create youth soccer fields. In 2003, the company built a 12-plex indoor theater on the old Twin site.

66 Drive-In

Opened: June 6, 1952

Closed: Sept. 1, 1986

Capacity: 1200 cars

Location: On Route 66, of course, on the south side of town.

The growing success of the Springfield Drive-In prompted the Kerasotes Theater chain to build its own

The 66 was huge. Even with its large screen, I wonder what the movie looked like to patrons sitting in those far back rows. Undated photo from the Sangamon Valley Collection at Lincoln Library, Springfield IL.

version, every bit as large as its competitor. And it was huge. The 66's curved screen, reportedly the largest in the state, was seven stories high and 80 feet wide, sitting 400 feet away from the projection building. The drive-in boasted 1307 RCA speakers, although some may have been for a seating area near the concession stand.

Kerasotes added a few tweaks after the grand opening. Before the end of the 1952 season, it had added a playground in front of the screen, later supplemented by a miniature train, a Ferris wheel, and an electric merry-go-round. During the 66's first off-season, Kerasotes installed 16-foot-high neon 6s on the back of the screen tower next to six-foot "drive-in theatre" letters. In the summer of 1955, it widened the screen to 120 feet for CinemaScope films. A 1957 remodeling included a shiny plastic coating to the new screen, plus upgrading the concession stand with air conditioning and pizza ovens.

Although this picture gives some idea of the glittery lights in the 66 shield, it doesn't convey the size of the marquee, which stood 20 feet high. 1980 photo from the Sangamon Valley Collection at Lincoln Library, Springfield IL.

And that was pretty much the end of the excitement. The 66 lived a quiet life, owned by Kerasotes through its final movie – *Reform School Girls* – at the end of the 1986 season. The next year, a Super 8 motel opened on the former 66 site, and it used the screen tower as an advertisement facing I-55. Fire damaged that screen tower in August 1991, and what was left was razed soon after. The motel was later remodeled into a Comfort Inn.

Green Meadows / Route 66 Drive-In

Opened: March 8, 1974

~~**Closed:** August 9, 1980~~ active

Capacity: 875 cars

Location: Just south of I-72, about two miles west of Business Route 66.

St. Louis-based Mid-America Theatres, which already owned at least a half-dozen Illinois drive-ins, moved into the Springfield market with a groundbreaking in March 1973. Mid-America announced that the twin-screen Green Meadows Drive-In, part of the Green Meadows Recreation Park, would open that summer. As it turned out, the drive-in didn't get finished until too late in the year to open.

A two-story concession-projection building was the heart of the Green Meadows, overlooking two smaller viewing fields where every pole had in-car speakers and heaters. That

The former Green Meadows added a nice touch of neon to its Route 66 Drive-In sign. 2017 photo from The BigScreen Cinema Guide (www.bigscreen.com). Copyright © SVJ Designs, LLC. All rights reserved.

drive-in ran for just seven seasons before becoming Springfield's first drive-in to fail, closing abruptly in the second week of August 1980.

Next door to the drive-in, George and Audrey Knight owned an amusement complex called Knight's Action Park. The family bought the closed Green Meadows, reopened one screen for one night (Oct. 6, 1990) to show *The Rocky Horror Picture Show*, and then tore down the second screen in 1991. A decade later, George's son Doug Knight painted the remaining screen, brought in over 6000 tons of gravel, and modernized the rest rooms. The younger Knight, who had grown up attending Springfield's former 66 Drive-In, reopened the Green Meadows as the Route 66 for the 2002 season. He rebuilt a second screen in 2004, and both screens are still active today.

Litchfield

To get a full, nostalgic experience of Route 66 in one place, my vote would be for Litchfield. It's got a very nice Route 66 Welcome Center. Across the street is the Ariston Cafe, one of the oldest surviving restaurants on the Mother Road. And just a stone's throw away is one of the few active drive-ins in this book.

Sky View Drive-In

Opened: June 22, 1950

~~Closed:~~ active

Capacity: 507 cars

Location: One block east of Route 66, on the north side of town.

The Frisina Amusement Company of Springfield IL began building the future Sky View in November 1949. It opened in the spring of 1950, but the exact date is fuzzy. *Boxoffice*, which sometimes had to write news stories days in advance, reported in successive months that the Sky View opened in mid-May, then on June 22, then in the first week of July. *Boxoffice* also wrote that the opening had been delayed week to week by bad weather.

The new drive-in covered 16 acres. The concession stand was separated from the projection building by a breezeway. The Sky View's screen was 42x52 feet, framed by a screen tower which was 55x65 feet. Two lighted pylons showed the drive-in's name in neon over large

The Sky View's marquee now includes a For Sale sign, though it's still open. 2021 photo by the author.

block letters, and a huge neon shooting star trailed more lines of neon behind it.

A tornado knocked down that screen tower in August 1974, so Frisina replaced it with a standard thin metal screen. Mid America Theaters, based in Sharon Springs KS, bought the Sky View along with 25 other Frisina theaters in October 1981. Just a few years later, Mid America sold the drive-in to Norman and Del Paul, and their family ran the Sky View for over 30 years.

The Pastrovich family, Nick and Mindy plus Nick's parents Mike and Debbie, bought the Sky View from the Paul family in March 2016. At the time, Mindy told Route66News.com, "We plan to run it as a drive-in indefinitely." Now the drive-in is for sale; Mindy said in a 2021 YouTube video that a severe auto accident made her reassess her work-life balance. "We'd like to see somebody come in here and love this as much as we have," she said. At press time, the asking price was $395,000, though the drive-in's web site said it planned to reopen again for the 2022 season.

Mount Olive

Little Mount Olive might be best known for its Union Miners Cemetery, the final resting place of labor organizer Mary "Mother" Jones. It's also the home of the Soulsby Service Station, the oldest surviving gas station on Route 66, restored but no longer in service.

Sunset Drive-In

Opened: June? 1951

Closed: 1975?

Capacity: 276 cars

Location: Just west of town on Route 66.

The details of the Sunset's origins are unusually vague. Trade publications announced in early summer of 1949 that Louis Odorizzi was going to build a 400-car drive-in on US 66 west of Mount Olive. In December 1949, the Macoupin County Board of Supervisors approved a petition for land "in the vicinity of the new drive-in theater near Mt. Olive". But 1950 brought no news, and in a February 1951 *Boxoffice* list of drive-in projects, the unnamed Odozizzi drive-in had yet to open.

Then there was the name. *The Exhibitor* wrote in May 1951 that the "Mount Olive Drive-In" would open soon, and *Boxoffice* later concurred with a June 16 scheduled opener. On July 21, *Boxoffice* wrote that the "Starlite Drive-In ... was opened recently." But all references soon changed to the drive-in's name to Sunset.

Reportedly, Louis did most of the jobs at his small drive-in, and his wife Edna ran the concession stand. Industry drive-in lists included the Sunset with a capacity of 276 cars, a figure that better matches its aerial photos. Odorizzi widened the east-facing screen in 1955,

A dozen concrete and metal stubs of the Sunset's old screen tower still sit today in a small grassy field between a VFW hall and old Route 66. 2021 photo by the author.

and a February 1973 aerial photo showed the drive-in still intact. That's about all I know for sure.

When did the Sunset close? Odorizzi passed away in April 1976, and it's easy to guess that the drive-in never reopened after that. A second theory comes from his nephew, who told the *Chicago Sun-Times* that "when I-55 came through, sweeping away their customers, they closed up." (The 1973 official Illinois highway map showed I-55 under construction by Mount Olive.) Finally, an internet user commenting on a photo of the gas station across Route 66 wrote, "There was also a drive in across the road from this. That was taken out by a tornado".

Today a VFW hall occupies the east side of the old Sunset site. A gently sloping gravel parking lot, two faint rows of grassy ramps, and the stubs of the old screen supports make it easy to sit in a car and imagine what it must have been like to watch a movie there.

Pontoon Beach

The village of Pontoon Beach, named for a sandy beach on Long Lake, incorporated in 1962, years after its drive-in had been built. Most contemporary mentions of the Bel-Air said it was in Granite City, which is now a stone's throw away, but the site is technically within Pontoon Beach's borders.

Bel-Air Drive-In

Opened: Dec. 25, 1953

Closed: August 1986

Capacity: 700 cars

Location: On Route 66 (now Chain of Rocks Road) at State Highway 111, about five miles east of the Chain of Rocks Bridge.

Louis Jablonow was general manager of what was then Komm Theaters when the company began construction on its second drive-in (after the Mounds, see below) in July 1953. Nearby residents were invited to suggest names; there's no record of whether the winning entry was inspired by the Chevrolet model, Los Angeles's exclusive neighborhood, or the earlier drive-in southwest of Chicago.

The Bel-Air opened on Christmas Day, a rare choice in a cold-weather climate, with Santa on hand to distribute toys to the children in attendance. A week later, it staged a dusk-to-dawn show for New Year's Eve. Both occasions gave the drive-in a chance to exercise its in-car heaters and a 200-person indoor "theatrette," air-conditioned in the summer months. Jablonow later said he believed it was the first drive-in with such an elaborate cafeteria-style concession building.

The deteriorating Bel-Air sign was a Route 66 icon for decades before it was sold and dismantled weeks after this 2018 photo by Steve Walser, used by permission.

As its owner' name changed to Jablonow-Komm, then Mid America Theatres, the drive-in rolled along. One night in 1961, a magnesium fire in a tractor-trailer truck on the highway was so bright that the Bel-Air stopped the movie for a half hour. In 1966, two teenagers who had been asked to leave the theatrette were arrested after hitting the manager with a piece of metal tubing.

Mid America added a second screen in May 1979, but shut down the drive-in on the week before Labor Day 1986. They quickly razed the site but left the distinctive two-sided bell sign, which became a nostalgic landmark for decades of Route 66 fandom. In 2018, a developer needed the space, so he dismantled the sign and sold it to two collectors. All that's left today is a short street that runs through the site. It's called Bel Air Drive.

Collinsville

The self-proclaimed "Horseradish Capital of the World" may be best known to Route 66 fans as the home of the 70-foot-high water tower called "The World's Largest Catsup Bottle®," which was built the same year as the city's drive-in.

Mounds / Falcon Drive-In

Opened: July 1, 1949

Closed: Jan. 16, 1983

Capacity: 700 cars

Location: West of Collinsville, about two miles west of Fairmount Park Race Track. In 1957, Route 66 shifted to Collinsville Road, bringing the Mother Road to the Mounds' entrance.

The Cahokia Mounds World Heritage Site was a prehistoric complex that was home to thousands of Native Americans. In the late 1940s, a group of businessmen thought that it would also be a great place to build a drive-in. In the summer of 1949, the Pimes Company, formed for the endeavor, opened the Mounds Drive-In within view of the 100-foot-high Monks Mound, reportedly flattening a couple of smaller mounds to make room. Later that year, the Komm theater circuit signed a 10-year lease to run the drive-in.

The Mounds occasionally ran what passed for racy films in the 1950s; in 1959 the East St. Louis chapter of the Knights of Columbus threatened a boycott over the drive-in's "immoral and obscene motion pictures." Mid America Theatres, the renamed Jablonow-Komm company, bought the Mounds in February 1960, promising "strictly family type" movies. Keeping with its theme of automobile names, Mid America renamed the drive-in the Falcon.

By the 1980s, as drive-ins everywhere looked for profitable films, the Falcon often turned to explicit X-rated movies. Its final triple feature included *Talk Dirty to Me Part 2* and *Getting Off*. That was in January 1983, when Illinois bought the drive-in to expand its Mounds State Historic Site. Today, a playground sits where the Falcon's ticket booth had been.

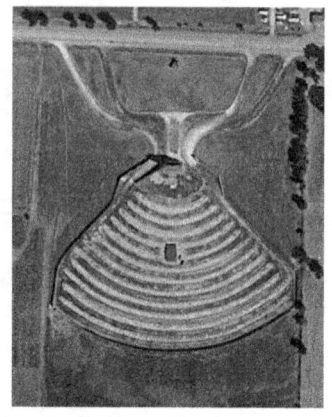

Can you see the playground area in front of the screen? 1955 photo © HistoricAerials.com, used by permission.

East St. Louis

In 1950, East St. Louis was the fourth-most populous city in Illinois, supported by heavy industry and railroads. The subsequent loss of those industries and other factors sent the city into a downward economic spiral, from which it is still working to recover. Other East St. Louis drive-in over three miles from Route 66: East St. Louis / French Village (1942-1984).

Shop City Drive-In

Opened: March 16, 1956

Closed: Sept. 1, 1980

Capacity: 600 cars

Location: Just off then-US 50, now St. Clair Avenue, about 2.6 miles east of 10th Street, which was City US 66 when the drive-in opened.

Illinois

Shop City, on the east side of East St. Louis, was supposed to boost the city's economy. It included both a shopping center and a new drive-in theater, built by Jablonow-Komm Theaters. Construction began in the summer of 1955, though it was held up for a month by a strike by carpenters and sheet metal workers. After the delays pushed the project past good weather that year, the Shop City opened at the first sign of spring in 1956.

At the time, the drive-in, which cost over a quarter-million dollars, was reported to be the first to be built as part of a shopping center complex. Just a few months after it opened, it filed an antitrust suit claiming studios were conspiring to withhold movies from the drive-in until after the local indoor theater had showed them.

In 1957, manager R. L. Weseman ran a "Lucky Speaker Post" contest for three months, hosted a live talent show as a benefit for area flood relief, and recruited radio disc jockey Bob Farrell for twilight record shows on weekends. On July 19, 1970, a wind storm demolished the Shop City's 75-foot-high screen, but the owners soon built a replacement. The drive-in lasted another decade, closing on Labor Day 1980. Most of the

The Shop City's grand opening ad in the *Belleville News-Democrat* featured a picture of its "self-service snack bar," as if that would be the big reason to visit the new drive-in.

viewing field was carved off for a nursing home, now closed. The remains of the screen still stand in a wooded area behind Clyde Jordan Stadium, the East St. Louis High School football field.

Intermission

Route 66 paths through greater St. Louis

The history of US 66 as it negotiated the St. Louis area is so convoluted that it was the sole subject of a 15-page article by James R. Powell in the Winter 1996 issue of *Show Me Route 66*, the Route 66 Association's quarterly magazine. Nothing can match the detail of that work, still available online at this writing. Using broader strokes, I'll try to give you a relevant summary.

When US 66 first arrived in 1926 it went through Edwardsville IL, crossed the Mississippi River at the McKinley Bridge, and went past Forest Park to Manchester Road and points west. Around 1929, it shifted to the Municipal "Free" Bridge, and the McKinley Bridge route became "Optional" (or Alternate) 66. In 1933, the highways were rerouted. US 66 went down Watson Road to the Municipal Bridge, while Optional 66 took Watson to the McKinley Bridge.

The iconic Chain of Rocks Bridge got involved in 1936, when US 66 ran across it and along Lindbergh Boulevard (then State Highway 77) around St. Louis to Watson Road, the west's first cloverleaf interchange. The previous route over the Municipal Bridge became City 66. Optional 66 stayed unchanged until it was discontinued a year later. On the Illinois side, City 66 shifted to go through East St. Louis.

Illinois

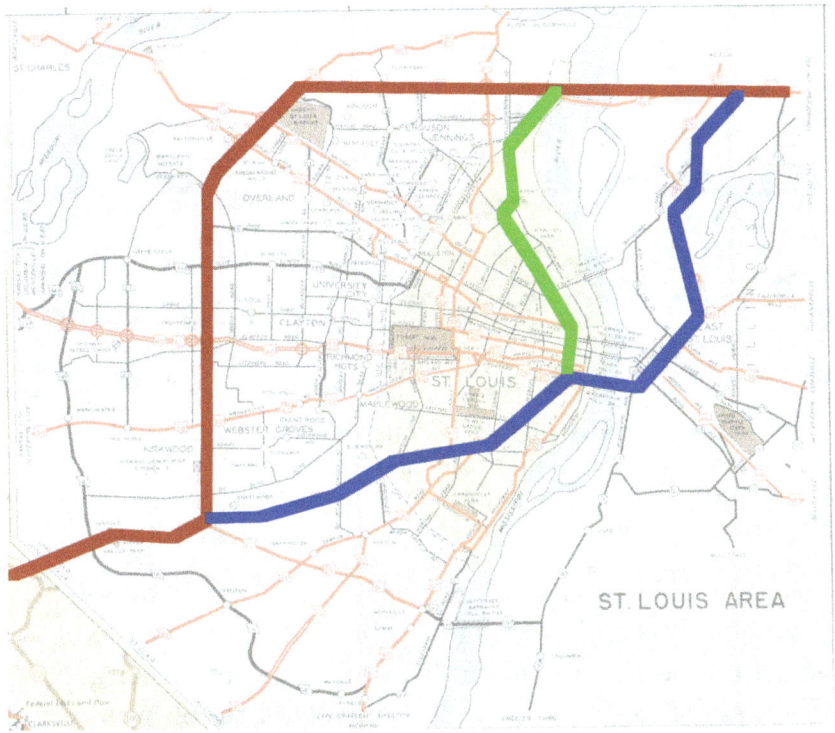

The main paths for Route 66 in the drive-in era. The red path shows it crossing the Chain of Rocks Bridge and circling St. Louis on the future Lindbergh Boulevard. The green path is where City 66 turned left after the bridge and dropped south through downtown. The blue path follows US 66 through East St. Louis, across a downtown bridge, and southwest on Watson Road.

From 1938 to 1955, the era when most of the area's drive-ins were built, those versions of Route 66 stayed put. When expressways began nosing into the region, they shifted again. The old route across the Chain of Rocks Bridge and around town on Lindbergh would be the "By-Pass Route," and a version that headed south from the Chain of Rocks Bridge to downtown would be the "City Route." City 66 would be renamed Business 66 before being eliminated in 1963.

The first cloverleaf highway connection in the west was in the southwest St. Louis area where US 66 met "By-Pass 66," and 50, 61, & 67 were in there too. 1957 Missouri Department of Transportation photo from the Missouri State Archives.

On the Illinois side, in 1961, the Mother Road joined newly-built I-55/70 north of Collinsville, and the next year followed it north of Fairmount Park, bypassing Collinsville Road. Back in St. Louis, By-Pass 66 was decertified in 1965, with Missouri authorizing removal of the signs in August.

US 66 was officially decertified from Chicago to Joplin in 1974, though Missouri kept 66 shields under I-44 markers for another two years.

To summarize, in the drive-in era, there are just three paths of concern. Going from east to west, one path from Illinois stayed on the north side, crossed the Chain of Rocks Bridge and followed Lindbergh all the way around to Watson Road. A second path dropped south near Collinsville and through East St. Louis, crossing at a downtown bridge and heading southwest, mostly along Watson Road. A third path, the short-lived City/Business Route, turned south immediately after crossing the Chain of Rocks, then stayed close to the river before rejoining the main route in downtown St. Louis. And that's our next stop on the Mother Road.

Missouri

In addition to being the Show-Me State, Missouri is also the Cave State, with over 6000 caves within its borders. Many of them are a short distance from Route 66. Meramec Caverns is the most famous example, and others include Onondaga Cave (about six miles south of the Leasburg exit) and Fantastic Caverns (four miles northwest of Springfield).

St. Louis

St. Louis differs from Chicago in two ways (at least): St. Louis embraced drive-ins very early on, and Route 66 didn't have a single, simple path through town. Some of its many routes included the iconic Chain of Rocks Bridge, now part of the Route 66 Bikeway.

St. Louis drive-in more than three miles from Route 66: South Twin (1954-1983). In nearby Pagedale: Olympic / Rock Road (1962-1980). Florissant's 270 Drive-In (1965-1980) opened days after "By-Pass 66" signs were removed from I-270.

Thunderbird Drive-In

Opened: July 3, 1959

Closed: Oct. 30, 1977

Capacity: 800 cars

Location: Just south of Natural Bridge Road, about two miles southwest of Florissant Avenue when it was Business Route 66.

In the 1950s and 60s, Louis Jablonow and his Jablonow-Komm Theatres kept looking to expand their circuit of profitable drive-in theaters. Along the way, they built the Thunderbird, the first St. Louis-area ozoner to use a double-ramp system. Its entrance on Natural Bridge was near another St. Louis landmark, the Goody Goody Diner.

The Thunderbird squeezed 800 parking spaces into a compact lot by using arcs of double ramps and by placing the projection-concession stand at the rear corner. 1968 photo © HistoricAerials.com, used by permission.

The same company, which eventually changed its name to Mid America Theatres, owned the drive-in for all of its life. Though not officially segregated, the Thunderbird's neighborhood was predominantly African-American. Through the 1970s, the drive-in showed more than its share of blaxploitation films; on one weekend in 1976, the double feature included the hit films *Sparkle* and *Cleopatra Jones*. The Thunderbird closed at the end of the 1977 season and never reopened in 1978. Nothing remains of the drive-in today.

Broadway Drive-In

Opened: May 30, 1954

Closed: Oct. 18, 1964

Capacity: 800 cars and 300 seats

Location: On Broadway about 1.3 miles southeast of Gravois Avenue when it was Route 66.

By 1953, Brentwood mayor A. Ray Parker saw the writing on the wall. He owned the Skyline Drive-In across the street from Lambert-St. Louis Municipal Airport, which was planning to expand. So Parker shifted his attention to a new drive-in, the first to be built within the St. Louis city limits. As it turned out, the Broadway's lifespan would only be a few months longer than the Skyline's.

The Broadway featured a "panoramic" 80x50-foot screen, which could handle the first wave of CinemaScope films. It was built with a playground and a seating area for walk-ins. In its early years, the lot was sometimes used as a park-and-ride lot for downtown commuters.

My favorite detail of the Broadway is that it faced a city jail. While building the drive-in, Parker ran a speaker line to the warden's residence on the second floor so he could enjoy free movies through his picture window.

Between its grand opening ad in the *St. Louis Post-Dispatch* and Cinema-Treasures user MitchWolf's April 1960 photo, we have a couple of glimpses of what the Broadway looked like.

In the end, another public project required Parker's land. This time, it was the construction of I-55. The Broadway closed after the 1964 season. Parker later became an executive vice president and general manager of Wehrenberg Theatres before retiring in 1983.

Jennings

James Jennings bought a huge tract of land here in 1839, then moved his family and slaves to start farming it. The city incorporated in 1946 on about the same borders as Jennings' farm. Its main attraction was the Northland Shopping Center, one of the first suburban malls in the St. Louis area.

North Drive-In

Opened: Sept. 17, 1948

Closed: Sept. 16, 2001

Capacity: 1200 cars

Location: On northern Lewis and Clark Boulevard, about 1.2 miles west of Riverview Drive when it was Business Route 66.

Clarence Kaimann was a St. Louis theater man who often partnered with Fred Wehrenberg. By the 1940s, they ran a couple dozen indoor theaters. Their only drive-in collaboration came just a few months after Wehrenberg had built Ronnie's and purchased the 66. The North Drive-In opened with a single screen and a lot that held 1000 cars.

That single screen was widened in 1954 to 102x62 feet, and the in-car speakers were upgraded to handle stereo sound. In 1955, the drive-in got a fresh set of in-car heaters to lengthen its season. In the 1960s, the Wehrenberg side of the business took over Kaimann's share of the North.

The drive-in's biggest change came in the spring of 1974, when it converted to the North Twin with the addition of a smaller second screen. Wehrenberg Theatres president Ron Krueger also expanded the concession stand to triple its original size, and somehow this was all done while the North showed movies every night.

The North Twin was the only St. Louis County drive-in to survive into the new millennium. After closing it at the end of the 2001 season, Wehrenberg sold the drive-in to real estate developers the following February. Tightly packed houses occupy the site today.

Wehrenberg Theatres transformed the North's viewing field in 1974 when it added a second screen. 1958 & 2002 photos © HistoricAerials.com, used by permission.

Crestwood

Ulysses Grant, future Civil War general and US president, lived in Crestwood in the 1850s when it was still a farm community. When Route 66 realigned along

Watson Road, it ran through the heart of the city. Crestwood's population exploded in the 1950s, growing from about 1600 at the start of the decade to over 11,000 in 1960.

66 Park-In

Opened: Sept. 26, 1947

Closed: Oct. 17, 1993

Capacity: 1200 cars

Location: On Route 66 just east of Sappington (now Old Sappington) Road.

In 1947, David Flexer of Memphis's Flexer Theatres set out on an ambitious schedule of building 25 "automobile movie theaters" throughout the country within two years. He managed at least two that year –

1958 photo courtesy of the Missouri State Archives, Department of Economic Development, Commerce and Industrial Development (CID) Division Collection.

1988 photo by John Margolies, John Margolies Roadside America photograph archive (1972-2008), Library of Congress, Prints and Photographs Division.

one in the Minneapolis area and the 66 Park-In, which opened in September. The reason that neither Flexer's press releases nor his theaters mentioned the word "drive-in" was probably because he didn't license Richard Hollingshead's ramp patent, nominally in effect at the time. Since Hollingshead's company sued Flexer in January 1948, I feel confident about that theory.

Fred Wehrenberg, head of St. Louis's Wehrenberg Theatres, came to the rescue, buying the 66 before it reopened for its second season in April 1948. (A Minnesota consortium bought Flexer's other "automobile theater" a week later.) St. Louis architect William Mills designed the 66, and it fit so well with the later Wehrenberg drive-ins that I'd guess Mills designed a few of them too.

When it opened, the 66 Park-In had a 56x60-foot screen and could hold 800 cars on its 18-acre lot. Its individual speakers were "placed inside the automobile by an attendant," according to Flexer's press release. In

1991 photo by Shellee Graham. Public domain. Courtesy of the Missouri State Archives, RG005 Secretary of State Publications Vanishing Missouri Photograph Collection.

1954, Wehrenberg installed an 80x40-foot wide screen, and also leased another 200 feet in the back of the lot to expand its capacity to 1200 cars.

The rest of the 66's life was as an iconic Mother Road landmark under quiet corporate ownership. It closed at the end of the 1993 season, and despite strong attendance, the Wehrenberg chain sold the Park-In for redevelopment. A shopping center occupies the site today.

Des Peres

Reported to be the oldest European settlement in Missouri, Des Peres was named by the French for the Catholic missionaries there. Centuries later, when the city hosted the state's first drive-in theater, Des Peres held fewer than 1000 residents. By the time the Manchester closed, more than 5000 lived in the city.

Most of the first wave of licensed drive-ins were known simply as "Drive-In Theatre." 1945 photo by Charles Trefts, courtesy of the State Historical Society of Missouri.

Manchester Drive-In

Opened: May 24, 1940

Closed: June 18, 1967

Capacity: 900 cars

Location: On Manchester Road after it had ceased to be Route 66, but 2.2 miles west of Lindbergh Boulevard when it was Bypass 66.

Philip Smith of Boston came to the St. Louis area in early 1940 to build its first drive-in theater. As was common for early ozoners, its name was simply "Drive-In Theatre." From the time it opened, the drive-in was an eye-opening hit, although these pioneers were still learning what worked. The drive-in's sound system consisted of 250 concrete pillars instead of posts, each with a speaker which provided sound for two cars.

The concession-projection building of the future Manchester, surrounded by some of the drive-in's speaker boxes. 1945 photo by Charles Trefts, courtesy of the State Historical Society of Missouri.

Some early news reports focused on the drive-in's benefits to invalids; one local doctor said, "Years of constant care and treatment have had less effect on two of my patients than several visits to the Drive-In, where they had suddenly discovered a new interest in life, the taken-for granted movie."

April 1941 brought Missouri's first drive-in Easter service, and management added a children's playground with a few swings. The refreshment stand grew from a simple popcorn seller to something closer to a modern concession area. Then World War II hit, and gasoline rationing prevented many of its patrons from driving to the movies.

In 1949, after the arrival of several other St. Louis County drive-ins, the original outdoor theater on Manchester Road became known as the Manchester Drive-In. Before the start of the 1954 season, the Manchester widened its screen to 50x102 feet and added three ramps to grow its capacity to about 900 cars.

From at least 1957 through 1965, the Manchester held weekly amateur talent shows during the summer.

Several winners were selected to take part in productions at the St. Louis Municipal Opera. By 1966, amid growing demand for shopping centers, management knew the Manchester's days were numbered. It closed in mid-summer 1967 and was replaced by the West County Shopping Center.

Bridgeton

Bridgeton was already a transportation hub before hosting both the St. Louis airport and a chunk of Route 66. It was near a ferry across the Missouri River; in the 1800s, wagons destined for the Oregon and Santa Fe Trails would pass through Bridgeton. When its drive-in was built, only about 200 people lived in the city. When it closed a decade later, the population had grown to over 7800.

Skyline Drive-In

Opened: June 21, 1950

Closed: Jan. 31, 1960

Capacity: 650 cars and 20 seats

Location: On what was then Natural Bridge Road, less than a mile east of Lindbergh Boulevard when it was Bypass 66.

Ray Parker spent months lining up the financing and land to build the Skyline across from Lambert Field, but finally got it open in the summer of 1950. In addition to the standard in-car speakers, the drive-in's playground featured a pony cart ride for children.

There was a big fuss in late 1950 when the Skyline advertised the "facts of life" movie *Mom and Dad*. St.

Ray Parker put his name at the top of the screen tower sign. 1951 photo by T. W. Kines for a drive-in theater study by the American Association of State Highway Officials.

Louis County officials prevented the Skyline from showing it, and the film's producers unsuccessfully attempted to get an injunction to allow it to be performed. The producers appealed to district court in January and it must have worked out, because the film played at the Skyline for a week in November 1951. Meanwhile, in April 1951, Parker was elected mayor of Brentwood.

As early as April 1954, trade publications began reporting that "Parker's Skyline Drive-In" (as it was written on the screen tower) would need to close soon to make way for airport expansion. Perhaps that's why Parker built the Broadway Drive-In that year.

Herbert Hartstein leased the Skyline from Parker in 1958. On Sept. 1 that year, lightning hit the screen and started a fire that caused heavy damage. But the drive-in quickly rebuilt the screen, reopened on Oct. 3 and continued showing movies until its last show on Jan 31, 1960. The site was swallowed up by the expanding airport; the American Airlines Ground Operations Center now sits where the Skyline's playground used to be.

St. Ann

Charles Vatterott started the community of St. Ann as a housing project for defense plant workers and their families. It incorporated as a city in 1948, and it expanded its boundaries in 1950 to include the Airway Drive-In. St. Ann's most prominent feature was Northwest Plaza, which became the largest enclosed shopping center in Missouri. The mall opened in 1965, expanded and enclosed itself in 1989, and closed in 2010.

Airway Drive-In

Opened: Sept. 21, 1948

Closed: Nov. 2, 1986

Capacity: 1000 cars and 1000 seats

Location: On St. Charles Rock Road less than a mile east of Lindbergh Boulevard when it was Bypass 66.

Henry Halloway of Halloway Theatres Corp., which operated a half-dozen indoor theaters in St. Louis County, announced in August 1947 that construction was underway on a large drive-in. For some reason, the Airway's grand opening was delayed by over a year from that point, longer than Halloway ran the drive-in.

In June 1949, Midwest Drive-In Theatres, a Boston-based company owned by Philip Smith, bought the Airway and took over its 30-year lease. By September that year, the drive-in offered pony rides and mini-automobiles for the children and 1000 stadium-style seats. Manager Sidney Sayetta told the *St. Louis Globe-Democrat* that, "Because it is located in a well-lighted area, the Airway has a high percentage of "walk-in" patrons."

The Airway's sign featured a majorette twirling a baton. © Joe Sohm | Dreamstime.com.

Sayetta was big on entertaining kids. He bought a 1921 pump truck from a nearby fire department and used it to drive children around the lot. He also formed a "1,000 Stadium Seat" club for kids under 12 in association with the St. Ann Lions Club, which supplied transportation for youngsters to the drive-in. In 1954, the Airway widened its screen and revamped the concessions stand.

Midwest Drive-In eventually became General Cinema Corp., and that's who sold the Airway to Wehrenberg Theatres in September 1974. Wehrenberg almost immediately began work to add a second screen, renaming the drive-in the Airway Twin on May 21, 1975.

Remember that lease? The land under the Airway Twin was bequeathed by the Halloway family to a set of 10 groups, mostly religious, which shared their lease payments of about $30,000 a year. By the early 1980s, the Airway Twin showed occasional X-rated movies, and the

St. Louis Post-Dispatch said the drive-in's physical plant was "deteriorating." Some of the religious groups that co-owned the land were embarrassed by the fact. In late 1986, a real estate man made a deal with Wehrenberg Theatres to end its lease on the Airway site early.

The Airway's neon sign, showing a marching band majorette with a twirling baton and kicking leg, was restored and repurposed as the sign for the Airway Shopping Center that took its place.

St. Ann 4-Screen Drive-In

Opened: June 2, 1951

Closed: Sept. 16, 1984

Capacity: 1000 cars

Location: On St. Charles Rock Road about a mile east of Lindbergh Boulevard when it was Bypass 66.

Los Angeles architect Eugene Wilson came up with an alternative design for a drive-in, built first in a Chicago suburb, second in St. Ann. Instead of one large screen, Wilson's version used four smaller screens, with two sets of projectors using mirrored lenses to cover two

By the time this sign photo appeared in the Oct. 6, 1951 issue of *Boxoffice*, the 4-Screen had already begun offering a choice of two double-feature programs.

This aerial view of the St. Ann 4-Screen Drive-In, with a glimpse of its marquee by the street, appeared in the June 8, 1959 issue of *Boxoffice*.

screens each. This way, cars could park closer to a screen and their passengers would have a shorter walk to the central concession-projection stand. The four smaller screens, each 30x40 feet, were easier to build and maintain than the typical five-story-high alternative. The design used rectangular areas of land very efficiently to maximize car capacity per acre. Personally, I think the concept was brilliant, but it never caught on. Not only weren't there more built, the Chicagoland drive-in converted to a standard single screen in 1955. There must have been downsides that aren't as obvious today.

Anyway, the St. Louis Amusement Company began building the 4-Screen in the second half of 1950. In March, it said completion was only a month away, but the grand opening slid another couple of months. When it first opened, it followed its Chicago-area brother in advertising all four screens with the same movie but with two staggered starting times. Before 1951 was over, the 4-Screen's ad featured "your choice of" two completely different programs. The drive-in's biggest draw seemed to be its coal-burning miniature train, which carried children and their families on six-minute rides over 1600 feet of track.

Before the show, a long line of children and their parents waited in front of the concession building for their turn on the 4-Screen's miniature train, as shown in the June 8, 1959, issue of *Boxoffice*.

In 1958, a *St. Louis Post-Dispatch* columnist described a night at the 4-Screen. The screens were labeled by color, including neon lights of red, blue, green, and yellow. Manager Marvin Stiver explained that without that color coding, patrons on their way back from the refreshment building would lose track of which screen their cars were facing.

By 1963, Arthur Enterprises ran the 4-Screen, and in October 1977, it lost control of the drive-in, reopened by Wehrenberg Theatres the following May. Throughout its life, it was sometimes called the St. Ann Drive-In, sometimes the St. Ann 4-Screen. It closed quietly at the end of the 1984 season and didn't open in 1985; a shopping center occupies the site today.

Overland

Daniel Boone built a one-room cabin in 1799 near the current location of Lake Sherwood. Travelers from St. Louis would stop at the "Overland Park" in the early 1800s. In 1919, the town's name was truncated to avoid confusion with Overland Park KS, and the city of Overland incorporated in 1939.

Holiday Drive-In

Opened: June 5, 1955

Closed: Sept. 1, 1985

Capacity: 1000 cars

Location: On Page Avenue about 1.5 miles east of Lindbergh Boulevard when it was Bypass 66.

Inspired by their success and lessons learned from their Mounds and Bel-Air drive-ins across the river in Illinois, Jablonow-Komm Theaters started work on their largest project in January 1955. The Holiday would feature 16 rows of cars between the projection booth and the screen, with 500 heaters for year-round operation. At a time when drive-in owners typically spent about $5000 to build a new concessions stand, company head Louis Jablonow invested $40,000

Shooting stars at the top and ground-based lights below drew attention to the Holiday, as shown in the July 2, 1955 issue of *Boxoffice*.

The Holiday put an unusual amount of emphasis on its patio dining area. Its owners hoped that the snack bar restaurant would also attract a lunch crowd. Photo from the July 2, 1955 issue of *Boxoffice*.

on the Holiday's. He accurately surmised that about 2/3 of patrons buy something to eat or drink, and 40 percent of the nightly sales were during the 20-minute intermission.

The oddest part of the concession stand was its location behind the back row of the huge theater. Jablonow put it there in the hope that he could appeal to Page Avenue lunch traffic, which was one reason it also boasted a paved patio with umbrella-covered tables and chairs. One of the byproducts of that choice was that the adjoining projection booth had reportedly the longest "throw" in the world – 730 feet to the 102-foot-wide screen. It took specially designed lenses to accomplish the feat.

Three more notes about that upfront building. The Holiday's playground area was next to the concession stand, and parents sometimes dropped off their kids there, found a parking spot, and then came back for them. The drive-in's restrooms were inside the concessions building, so patrons would have to walk past the tempting treats on the way to do their business. And speaking of business, Mid-America Theatres, the eventual name of the Jablonow chain, had its corporate headquarters on site.

Just before the 1976 season, Mid-America remodeled the Holiday, reopening as a twin on Feb. 6, then as a four-screen drive-in three weeks later. Unlike the 4-Screen in St. Ann, the Holiday showed different movies on all four of its screens. RKO bought the Mid-America chain from the Jablonow family in April 1984, then closed the Holiday less than two years later. A mall of small office buildings occupies the site today.

Sappington

Sappington, an unincorporated chunk of land, was named for settlers John and Jemima Sappington. In 1804, their family bought three square miles, a larger area than this census-designated place occupies today.

Ronnie's Drive-In

Opened: July 15, 1948

Closed: Sept. 12, 1982

Capacity: 1200 cars

Location: On South Lindbergh Boulevard about 2.3 miles south of Route 66 in Crestwood.

Fred Wehrenberg's first open-air theater was an Airdome, built before the Great Depression. The long-time St. Louis showman began building his second, a drive-in instead of a roofless lot with chairs, in August

1947. From the beginning, it was to be named Ronnie's after his grandson, Ronald Paul Krueger.

Although it had been originally planned to open at the start of the 1948 season, construction delays pushed the date back a couple of months. That was long enough for Wehrenberg Theatres to buy the nearby 66 Park-In earlier that year, so Ronnie's became the company's second drive-in.

Ron Krueger drove a mini-tractor for children's hay rides for "his" drive-in's first season. In 1954, his father Paul Krueger, a general manager for Wehrenberg, widened the screen from 66x68 feet to 102x72 feet to accommodate CinemaScope. Instead of attaching wings to the old screen, as many drive-ins did for widescreen movies, Krueger had workers attach a new screen to the old tower, allowing it to curve and tilt downward slightly. That year, he also added a second concessions building as part of an extra ramp, increasing Ronnie's capacity from 1000 cars to 1200.

The Wehrenberg Theatres' screen towers looked remarkably alike, as you can tell from Ronnie's grand opening ad in the *St. Louis Star and Times*.

The drive-in found profitable tie-ins. In 1959, packages of Mayrose Franks each contained a low-price carload ticket to one of a few Mayrose nights at Ronnie's. In 1962, Wehrenberg made a deal with local tour buses to use the drive-in's restrooms for potty breaks, while their tourists could also purchase food and drinks at the concession stand.

After his father passed away, Ron actually took charge of Ronnie's in 1964. He ripped out the old concession-projection building to build a much larger new one, which he equipped with the area's first 70/35mm projectors.

The Wehrenberg chain had discussed using Ronnie's land for an indoor theater complex as early as 1963. Twenty years later, bulldozers pulled down the screen tower, and the company built an eight-screen indoor movie house on the site. They later replaced that with a 20-plex, and that's what's still there today.

Valley Park

At the time the I-44 Drive-In was operating, it was in the small town of Peerless Park, which formed in 1935. In 1998, Peerless Park was disincorporated and annexed by the city of Valley Park. More recently in 2015, the Meramec River left its banks, covering the drive-in site and its adjacent rails and highways.

I-44 Drive-In

Opened: March 31, 1972

Closed: Sept. 23, 1984

Capacity: 850 cars

Location: Just north of the intersection of State Highway 141 and I-44, which was also Route 66 when the drive-in opened.

The I-44 was the last drive-in opened by Wehrenberg Theatres, named for the freshly completed interstate nearby. Its 100-foot screen faced 16 concentric ramps, plus another six acres left for an indoor theater that was never built. Three hundred of the I-44's parking spaces were equipped with in-car heaters for winter patronage.

The concession stand, placed in the middle of the back rows, had an exterior of charcoal gray accented in tangerine. Color on the inside was provided by green Formica countertops on twin cafeteria lines. The projection booth sat on the second floor of the building.

Though today it's less than two miles from a wooded bird sanctuary, the I-44 Drive-In site was in a flat, treeless valley. 1979 USGS aerial photo.

In the 1970s, the I-44 hosted occasional concerts; the rock band Styx once performed there. In 1982, radio station KSD sponsored the flea market at the I-44.

Tom Stockman of the "We Are Movie Geeks" blog wrote, "The I-44 had the worst location for a drive-in. It sat in the valley wedged between a landfill, railroad tracks, and the Meramec River." With river fog, mosquitoes, train noise, and the scent of a nearby landfill, it's a little surprising that the I-44 lasted for 13 seasons. Fittingly, a waste transfer station occupies the site today.

Sullivan

The small city of Sullivan straddles two counties, Franklin and Crawford. (The drive-in was in Franklin County.) It's the closest in this list to Route 66 icon Meramec Caverns, an enjoyable place for its collection of kitsch or its old-fashioned cave tour.

The top of the Grande's grand opening ad in the *Sullivan Tri-County News* gave readers a look the screen tower facing Route 66. The Grande had actually opened three weeks earlier.

Grande Drive-In

Opened: Aug. 22, 1952

Closed: 1983?

Capacity: 300 cars

Location: On Route 66 due north of Bottomley City Park.

In 1940, Russian immigrant Abe Schwartz built the Grande Courts, a collection of 12 tourist cottages and a gas station, on Route 66. In May 1952, he started building a drive-in just west of the cottages, and of course he named it the Grande Drive-In. Its 60-foot-high screen was built of over 10,000 concrete blocks. Some of the guests on the west side of those cottages could see the screen, but there's no evidence that Schwartz ever wired those adjacent rooms for sound. The Grande held a highly promoted grand opening on September 10, three weeks after it had opened to the public.

By 1955, the *Theatre Catalog* listed Lee Norton as the owner of the Grande. In 1957, *Motion Picture Exhibitor* wrote that Hugh Graham was operating the drive-in. By 1959, the drive-in was owned by the 19-year-old, ill-fated Tommy Shaffer.

The lucky guests in the northwest building of Abe Schwartz's Grande Courts could watch the movie from their rooms. But could they hear it? 1955 photo © HistoricAerials.com, used by permission.

On Oct. 2, 1959, a "baby tornado" hit Sullivan in general and the Grande in particular. The twister bent one of the drive-in's neon signs in two, wrecked the screen's wing walls, blew speakers from the back of the field to the front, and tore off a chunk of the roof of the concession stand. Despite all that damage, Shaffer showed his movies on schedule that evening. He replaced the screen the following May.

After the 1963 season, Shaffer disappeared while visiting St. Louis. His body was soon found, badly beaten and shot, in a brush patch about halfway between Sullivan and St. Louis. The New Grande Investment Corp. bought the drive-in, which was managed by Ted Siebenman in 1964 and Myron Woodcock in 1965.

The Grande hit the headlines once more in 1974. Its showing of *The Models*, an R-rated movie, provoked a picket line promoted by some of Sullivan's churches. Perhaps as a result, cars waiting to enter the drive-in lined up for more than a mile, and the drive-in enjoyed its best attendance in years.

I'm uncertain when the Grande closed. It operated into the 1980s, then was sold to J. Jaeger, who kept it going for one or two more years. The drive-in was gone by 1985. Today, Schwartz's cottages still stand, currently as a Motel 6. The drive-in was replaced by a restaurant and another motel.

Cuba

For Route 66 fans, Cuba is best known as the home of the Wagon Wheel Motel. It started in the 1930s as 14 stone cabins. John Mathis bought the cabins in 1947, added a building with another four units, and designed its famous neon sign. Today, Connie Echols owns the Wagon Wheel, the oldest continuously operated motel on the Mother Road.

19 Drive-In

Opened: June 1955

~~**Closed:**~~ active (?)

Capacity: 250 cars

Location: On State Highway 19 one mile north of Route 66, now just north of I-44.

Adolph Meier was born in St. Louis in 1910. After marrying the former Zeta Bousser in 1931, he moved to his new wife's home town of Cuba. Within a few years,

A few decorative speakers remain in the 19's viewing field. 2021 photo by the author.

he owned the indoor Cuba Theatre there, and Zeta was the cashier. In 1945, Meier sold the theater to Rowe Carney of Rolla; four years later, he bought it back from him.

In July 1952, Meier announced that he would build a 300-car drive-in a half mile from the Cuba city limits on US 66. I don't think that one ever opened, though a large cleared area on the east side of town was visible on aerial photos a few years later. Instead, Meier started building the 19 in April 1955, and opened it a couple of months later. It had a 36x72-foot screen and held about 200 cars. For at least some of the years he operated both theaters, Meier would close the indoor Cuba in the months the 19 was open and vice versa.

Don Spreng purchased the 19 in 1973. The drive-in added a couple of ramps in the back, increasing its capacity to about 250-300. Don and his wife Susan ran the

19, and by 2005, their grade-school daughters were helping out during the summer. The drive-in went on the market in 2012 after Don passed away, but Susan decided to keep the 19. She bought a new digital projector and installed daughter Karen in charge.

For the 2021 season, Karen Spreng paused the drive-in for a year, citing problems with repairs to the projector and concession stand. At press time, the 19's future remained uncertain.

Rolla

When its drive-in opened, Rolla was home to the Missouri School of Mines and Metallurgy. Since then, the school changed its name to the University of Missouri-Rolla, then to its present name, Missouri University of Science and Technology. Around 1861, Rolla's founders named it after Raleigh NC, but reportedly adopted the five-letter version because it was easier to spell.

Rolla Drive-In

Opened: Oct. 17, 1950

Closed: Aug. 31, 1986

Capacity: 500 cars

Location: On Route 66 about a mile north of town.

In 1949, the Hopkins family had a drive-in almost ready to open in Rolla, but not this one. After they had broken ground earlier that year, Rowe Carney, owner of the indoor theater in nearby Cuba MO, began building his own drive-in a half-mile closer to town. Carney was losing the construction race, but in the nick of time, he bought out the Hopkins drive-in and returned to his own project.

Missouri

Carney's site took a lot of heavy excavation work to prepare the viewing field; maybe that's why the drive-in screen, 38x50 feet and standing 60 feet high, didn't arrive until June 1950. Then a couple of months of heavy rains wore holes into the ramps before workers could cover the viewing field with gravel. Although the "Rolla DeLuxe Drive-In Theatre" didn't open until mid-October, unseasonably pleasant weather that weekend allowed for large crowds, directed by lighted runways and a crew of ushers.

Detail of a 1957 photo by the Missouri Department of Transportation, showing the Rolla Drive-In between the original US 66 and the freshly completed four-lane 66. Note the exposed screen tower supports. Photo courtesy of the Missouri State Archives.

By 1959, the back of the Rolla's screen tower was covered. Missouri Department of Transportation photo courtesy of the Missouri State Archives.

And that was most of the excitement for the Rolla, which was often advertised as simply "Drive-In Theatre." Missouri's highway department built a four-lane US 66 Bypass soon after the drive-in opened, but was kind enough to place it behind the screen. In the next few years, Carney acquired the city's indoor Ritz and Uptown theaters. He also developed a wide-screen movie format that he called Rotoscope (not related to the animation technique); some of his early movies included shots of his drive-in.

Before the 1971 season Commonwealth Theatres bought all three of the Carney theaters in Rolla. They remodeled the concession stand, and that seems to be about it. The Rolla Drive-In's last newspaper ad appeared on the weekend before Labor Day 1986. A 1987 aerial photo showed the drive-in still intact, but it probably didn't reopen that year. A car dealership occupies the site today.

St. Robert

Route 66 travelers on their way to Fort Leonard Wood would make the turn south in St. Robert. The city also hosts the George M. Reed Roadside Park, the only Mother Road-side park left in Missouri.

Woodlane Drive-In

Opened: April 1954?

Closed: 1986?

Capacity: 280 cars

Location: Less than half a mile south of Route 66 near the Fort Leonard Wood entrance.

The origins of the Woodlane are just a little fuzzy. *The Exhibitor* magazine wrote in October 1952 that Dave Forbes was building a similar-sized drive-in "on US 66 near Waynesville." (Every print reference to the Woodlane placed it in Waynesville, St. Robert's adjacent, larger city.) Was that project related to Commonwealth Theatres' under-construction announcement in February 1953?

The Woodlane was a short distance from the entrance to Fort Leonard Wood, the inspiration for the drive-in's unique name. 1958 photo by the Missouri Department of Transportation courtesy of the Missouri State Archives.

The next question is when the drive-in opened. *The Exhibitor* wrote on Aug. 26, 1953 that Commonwealth had opened a drive-in on 66 in Waynesville. In the following January's annual *Motion Picture Almanac*, Commonwealth's theater list included an unnamed drive-in in Waynesville. Yet the March 17, 1954 *Exhibitor* said, "The new drive-in being constructed on Highway 17, one-half mile south of the junction of Highway 17 and 66 at the Fort Wood entrance, Waynesville, Mo., is expected to open late this month". Then several trade publications carried the news of the Woodlane's grand opening in April.

Something catastrophic happened at the Woodlane around December 1954. *Motion Picture Herald* noted in its Christmas 1954 issue, "The recently constructed Woodlane drive-in theatre at Waynesville, Mo., and all sound and concession projection equipment was destroyed recently." The drive-in didn't reopen until July 1955, with the city's merchants running a full-page newspaper ad thanking its management.

Commonwealth Theatres owned the Woodlane for all of its life, which was mostly quiet except for a few times when it made the news. In July 1960, three AWOL soldiers killed the Woodlane's bookkeeper in an attempted robbery. The trigger man was sentenced to life in prison.

Another view of the Woodlane. 1955 photo © HistoricAerials.com, used by permission.

The drive-in lost its power one April evening in 1966. A single-engine plane flew low and erratically over US 66, and crashed on the 66 spur near the fort, trailing a power line from its tail. The pilot escaped with minor injuries but was charged with "flying an airplane too low while consuming intoxicating beverages." In October that year, a tornado ripped down the Woodlane's screen.

The Woodlane's closing date is also a little fuzzy. Its last appearance in the list of Commonwealth's holdings was in the 1987 *Motion Picture Almanac*, suggesting that it didn't reopen that spring. A car dealership occupies the site today.

Lebanon

This city was named for another place, but not the one you think – Lebanon TN, the former home of many of its founders. Lebanon MO is home to the Munger Moss Motel, a Route 66 icon that's still active today. Other Lebanon drive-ins more than three miles from Route 66: Mini 5 (1972-1988?), Moonlight (1949-1957?).

Ski-Hi Drive-In

Opened: July 2, 1952

Closed: 1982?

Capacity: 200 cars

Location: About 1.2 miles due west of Route 66 on the southwest side of town.

Earl Hargis, auctioneer and owner of the Ski-Hi Café in Lebanon, decided in 1952 to get into the movie business. Of course, he named his new drive-in after his restaurant. The tiny Ski-Hi held only 200 cars, and it had a manager's living quarters on the grounds.

What I know about the drive-in after its opening is incomplete, like looking at a scene through a picket fence. Hargis advertised the Ski-Hi for sale in April 1959, but the first notice that someone bought it was in the March 5, 1962 issue of *Boxoffice*, which said that Olen Barton of St. Louis was the new owner. Three weeks later, the magazine said that Barton had flipped the drive-in to Howard Thompson.

Most of the rest of my Ski-Hi info comes from the *Motion Picture Almanac*, which is so fallible that it listed Hargis as the owner through 1966. After a decade without owner data, the

As far as I can tell, the drive-in's grand opening ad in the *Lebanon Daily Record* was the only time it was spelled with a -gh at the end.

MPA wrote for its 1977-82 editions that F. Kennedy owned the Ski-Hi. A 1983 aerial photo showed that the drive-in was gone, but the 1983-84 *MPA* editions said that it had been replaced by the Sundowner, owned by R. Bethel. A thorough search of the local newspapers for those summers turned up no drive-ins, Sundowner or otherwise, so I'd say that the *MPA* got a wire crossed. A truck parts building occupies the site today.

Marshfield

Noted astronomer Edwin Hubble was born and raised in Marshfield. The city keeps a replica of the orbital Hubble Telescope on its courthouse lawn in his honor. Marshfield also has the highest elevation of any part of Route 66 within Missouri.

Skyline Drive-In

Opened: May? 1952

Closed: Sept. 3, 1955

Capacity: 200 cars

Location: On Route 66 about a mile east of town.

Lloyd Schmidt of nearby Niangua MO bought the Skyline Café from Herman Pearce in late 1951. Schmidt must have liked the name, because he opened the Skyline Drive-In the following spring at a different site, just over a mile northeast of downtown Marshfield. The drive-in sat on the south side of Route 66, its screen facing away from the highway.

Little is known about the Skyline. Its only surviving image is an aerial photo. *The Exhibitor* wrote in April 1952 that Schmidt was building the drive-in with Harold

Owen, a flying enthusiast and theater owner from Seymour MO who's only known tie to the Skyline was that one mention. The Skyline's first ad in the *Marshfield Mail* was on May 1, 1952, but it didn't say anything about a grand opening.

In July 1955, another Niangua resident, Dwight Cantrell, bought the Skyline from Schmidt. Cantrell ran the drive-in for the rest of the season. In the Skyline's final ad, before Labor Day weekend that year, he wrote, "This will be the final show at the Drive-In this year. We have appreciated the loyalty of our patrons." There is no evidence that the Skyline reopened after that.

This is the only known image of the tiny Skyline Drive-In. 1955 photo © HistoricAerials.com, used by permission.

A visitor to the Webster County Historical Museum in Marshfield recalled that the Skyline used loudspeakers instead of in-car speakers. That would be unusual but not unheard of in the early 1950s. A couple of houses occupy the site today.

Springfield

John Woodruff called Springfield "the crossroads of America" since US 65 and 66 met there. In 1925, he built the Woodruff Arms Hotel, one of the first to focus on automobile travelers. The next year, he worked with Cyrus Avery to found the US Highway 66 Association.

Other Springfield drive-ins more than three miles from Route 66: Hi-M (1961-1984), Queen City Twin (1974-1985).

The skeleton of the Holiday's sign still guards the drive-in's empty fields. 2021 photo by the author.

Holiday Drive-In

Opened: Aug. 13, 1970

Closed: Sept. 20, 1996

Capacity: 529 cars

Location: On Business Route 66, (Kearney Street), just over a mile east of town.

In the summer of 1968, Commonwealth Theatres began grading work on the first planned site for what would become the Holiday. By the following May, Commonwealth had abandoned that plan, choosing instead an open area about five miles north. Although Commonwealth announced that it would be a twin drive-in, and subsequently graded two viewing fields, when the Holiday finally opened in 1970, it had only the single screen it would keep for the rest of its life.

The Holiday led a typically quiet corporate existence until it closed at the end of the 1984 season. It then sat idle for almost a decade until Christopher Maples leased the land and reopened the Holiday on June 11, 1994. Using FM radio sound instead of in-car speakers, Maples kept the Holiday going for three more seasons, then it closed for good. The fields are vacant now, surrounded by trees, but the frame of the original Holiday sign is still visible from Kearney Street.

Springfield Drive-In

Opened: Aug. 19, 1947

Closed: Oct. 7, 1978

Capacity: 750 cars

Location: Just off US 65 about two miles south of its intersection with Business Route 66.

After years of managing what would become known as the Manchester Drive-In in Des Peres, Sam Taft looked to Springfield to build a drive-in of his own. Much like the place where he used to work, Taft's ozoner opened as "Drive-In Theater," but he installed in-car speakers from the start. After a quiet opening in August, Taft's new drive-in held its grand opening on Sept. 19.

It appears that Taft's business plan didn't work out. After the drive-in's first season, a cluster of builders and other businesses won judgments, possibly for unpaid bills, against the S. M. Taft Amusement Corp. Rush Wilhoit became the drive-in's court-appointed operator in April 1948, then Commonwealth Theatres swooped in during the following off-season to buy the Springfield, complete with a 30-year lease on the land.

The Springfield Drive-In had a playground with a mural at the base of the screen. Note the fenced-off area to the right; the projection building was very close to the screen. Photo from the April 10, 1961 issue of *Boxoffice*.

The Springfield had a quiet life under Commonwealth. In the 1976-77 off-season, the local manager rented the place for folks who wanted to sell their cars. In 1978, the refreshment stand offered fried fingers (deep fried hot dogs) and other ghoulish snacks during the run of *Blood Thirsty Butchers*. Then at the end of the season, coinciding with the end of its lease, the Springfield ended its life with a marathon of five Ma and Pa Kettle movies. Insurance offices occupy the site today.

Sunset Drive-In

Opened: July 21, 1950

Closed: Sept. 4, 1983

Capacity: 546 cars

Location: On Route 66 about two miles west of town.

Commonwealth Theatres must have liked the business it was seeing at the Springfield Drive-In, because it soon got to work on building the city's second drive-in. When it opened, the Sunset didn't have a playground, but Commonwealth added one later along with a court for pitching horseshoes.

Like its sister drive-in, the Sunset enjoyed a quiet life under Commonwealth management. In 1962, its manager ran a classified ad for "Man to be hypnotized and buried alive for 3 days and nights without food or water, at the Sunset Drive-In Theatre, Friday, July 20. Pleasant working conditions". In 1974, two teenagers fell asleep during the show and woke up under arrest for marijuana possession. The lighted sign on the highway was damaged a few times, and high winds knocked down the screen on May 30, 1977.

Above, the Sunset's layout as of 1959. Photo © HistoricAerials.com, used by permission. Below, in 1954, *Boxoffice* had a grainy glimpse of the Sunset's horseshoe court.

Despite these small setbacks, the Sunset endured, though it turned to R-rated movies more frequently in its declining years. The final program at the end of the 1983 season featured *Naked Weekend*, *Center Fold Girls*, *Senior Snatch*, and *Miss Nude America*. A mobile home park occupies the site today.

Carthage

This is the place where I first experienced Route 66. In the 1970s, I drove down old US 71 through the night on my way to the Ozarks. I remember arriving here before dawn as the city's north side first appeared as the spooky Garrison Street Overpass, complete with 1920s streetlights. After a few blocks of houses, I stopped for a red light. The bright intersection there felt somehow important and mundane, like an old movie star buying groceries. This was 71's crossing of Route 66, featuring large gas stations and the classic Boots Court, waiting to serve travelers even then.

Sunset Drive-In

Opened: August 1949

Closed: Sept. 23, 1973?

Capacity: 248 cars

Location: On Route 66 about a mile east of town.

Clyde Leeson ran the Sunset Café and had a few cabins at his place about a half mile east of Kellogg Lake. By 1946, visitors would congregate on his front yard, some still in their cars, to watch movies from a small projector on a 20x20-foot screen. He didn't charge admission, but he knew how well the movies drew hungry customers to his restaurant. In 1949, he made the arrangement more official, building a permanent screen and opening his Sunset Drive-In.

His son Bud, who worked the concession stand, later told the *Joplin Globe*, "You got to understand, we didn't have the individual car speakers. Dad just fixed up about four huge horns at the top of the screen for the sound to

This little stone building in front of the old Sunset site was built in 1935. There's also still a sign, now blank. Was it for the café, the drive-in, or the cabins? 2016 photo by Ken Bogren, courtesy of Route66Times.com

come out of. You couldn't sit on the front row, or you'd go deaf." Admission was just 50 cents a carload most nights, a full dollar on Saturdays, and some people just listened for free from the banks of Kellogg Lake.

In the Sunset's newspaper ads for July 4th weekends in 1971 and 1972, Leeson promised, "All the little kiddies that come to the drive-in will receive a big sack of fireworks free." In between those ads, he was admitted to the hospital, then put the drive-in up for sale "due to the health of owner." Apparently there were no buyers, and the Sunset's final ad was at the end of the 1973 season. Clyde passed away in 1981, and Bud founded Bud's Bait, still in business after 59 years. The ticket booth foundation is still visible at the Sunset site along with the remains of a small sign that might have been for the café, the drive-in, or both.

When this picture was taken around 2010, the 66 still showed some of the its screen tower supports. © Lightvision | Dreamstime.com

66 Drive-In

Opened: Sept. 22, 1949

~~**Closed:**~~ ~~1985~~ active

Capacity: 400 cars

Location: On Route 66, about two miles west of town.

William Bradfield, who owned the indoor Roxy in Carthage, got the idea in 1949 to build a drive-in nearby. He had hoped to open it by mid-September, but delays kept the 66 closed until the month was nearly done. As it was, one of the drive-in's sound amplifiers went quiet on opening night, and one of the two projectors' lights was too dim to show much on the screen. Bradfield corrected the problems by the following night.

The 66's screen tower was completely covered by 2019, when the author took this photo. It was featured on the cover of the first edition of this book.

The 66 rolled along under Bradfield's ownership for over a decade, until he sold it to Dickinson Theatres, effective April 1964. New manager Robert Klinge set up a Moon Maids promotion that September, with 100 area girls throwing paper plate "flying saucers" to the crowd. The Dickinson years were relatively quiet, even more so in 1985 when the 66 closed, seemingly for good. Brothers Robert and Mark Goodman bought the 66 to use as an auto parts junkyard.

As do-it-yourself auto repairs became more complicated in the 1990s, the owners recognized that the 66 would be more valuable as a reopened drive-in. Mark Goodman partnered with Wes Alumbaugh to restore the 66, a massive effort that included gutting the old concession stand to rebuild its interior from scratch. The better-than-new 66 reopened in late August 1997, and stayed with the Goodman family for the next 20 years.

Not only is the 66 Drive-In iconic and photogenic, it's also popular. On weekends, cars and light trucks can line up along the old highway waiting for the gates to open. Photo from The BigScreen Cinema Guide (www.bigscreen.com). Copyright © SVJ Designs, LLC. All rights reserved.

In 2017, Mark Goodman sold the 66 to Nathan McDonald and his family. McDonald, who had worked there for 10 years, told the *Carthage Press*, "I was very fortunate and honored enough for them to pass the torch to me and my family so we can carry it on and build on what they built." Today, the 66 is still going strong, a well-maintained international icon, included in the National Register of Historic Places.

Webb City

It's not a drive-in, but Mother Road film fans might want to check out the Route 66 Movie Theatre in downtown Webb City. Formerly the Dickinson Theatre, it sat idle for years before it was renovated in 1999 as the Route 66 Music Theatre. The current owners bought it in 2005 and restored it to a movie theater again.

Webb City Drive-In

Opened: June 26, 1953

Closed: Oct. 12, 1997

Capacity: 406 cars

Location: On Route 66 on the south side of town.

Howard Larsen, owner of the city's indoor Civic Theatre, got his permit to build a drive-in in February 1953 and went right to work. He rushed the opening of the Webb City in June, promising to add a playground and a lake stocked with fish. The playground arrived before the season was done, but I never read anything more about a fishing lake. Some patrons enjoyed the observation deck on the roof of the concession building. In September 1954, Larsen replaced the screen with a CinemaScope 75x40 footer.

William Bradfield, owner of Carthage MO's 66, bought the Webb City in 1956. Dickinson Theatres bought the Webb City, along with the 66 and an indoor theater, in a late 1963 deal effective April 1964. Dickinson then ran the Webb City for 34 seasons, 1964-1997.

One remarkable aspect of the Webb City was how little its sign changed over 40 years of service. Above is a photo from *Boxoffice* printed a few months after the drive-in opened. Below is a 1993 photo posted at CinemaTreasures.org by user moviejs1944.

Dickinson offered the Webb City for sale in 1995. Hollywood Theatres took over Dickinson's Joplin-area indoor theaters on Oct. 3, 1997. The Webb City was the last theater to stay under the Dickinson banner for one more weekend. Despite good attendance, Dickinson announced the sale of the drive-in to Wal-Mart the following spring, and that's what's still there today.

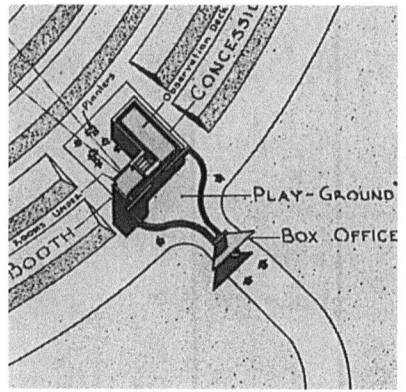

The Webb City had a protected playground area next to the concession stand, as shown in the Nov. 21, 1953 issue of *Boxoffice*.

Joplin

Route 66 fans in Joplin will want to check out the murals at the Pearl Brothers hardware store. The larger mural on top shows a classic blue-green sedan driving by a "Welcome to Joplin" sign, and the street-level mural features a map ribbon of the Mother Road with half of a (fake) 1964 Corvette embedded on the side.

Not included: Mini Drive-in, an Autoscope, (1971-1985). See the Intermission below.

Crest Drive-In

Opened: Aug. 7, 1952

Closed: Oct. 9, 1983

Capacity: 500 cars

Location: On US 71 two miles south of its intersection with Route 66, on the southeast side of town.

Missouri

Commonwealth clearly liked Joplin's response to its first drive-in, because it soon started work on its second. It also opened with a fireworks display. Its 500-car capacity was a little smaller than the Tri-State, and it opened with a 40x30-foot screen.

Jim Randall, the news director of a local radio station, was one of the 50 entrants in the contest to name Commonwealth's new drive-in. Randall's selection was the Crest, and he won a $25 bond and a season's pass for two. I'm not surprised that Commonwealth liked the name; it was building a Crest Drive-In in suburban Kansas City at the same time it built the Tri-State.

The Crest's grand opening ad as it appeared in the *Joplin Globe*. The drive-in also had a modern cafeteria-style concession stand with a window for watching the projectors.

A windstorm, probably a tornado, swept through in July 1964, picking up panels of the Crest's metal fence and dropping them 1000 feet away. In 1970, Commonwealth added an extra ramp to expand its capacity, restoring it to the 500 cars that it had claimed since it opened.

The Crest was the second drive-in to open in Joplin, but it was the first to close. A restaurant and a couple of car dealers occupy the site today.

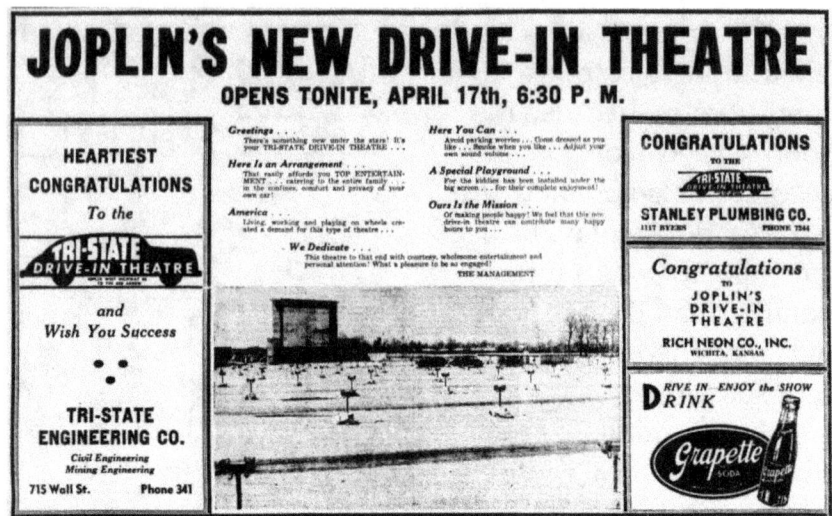

The top of the Tri-State's grand opening ad in the *Joplin Globe* included a view of the drive-in's viewing field.

Tri-State Drive-In

Opened: April 17, 1948

Closed: Sept. 4, 1988

Capacity: 625 cars

Location: On Route 66, next to Schifferdecker Golf Course on the west side of town.

When Commonwealth Theatres opened the region's first drive-in theater, it caused a big splash. With a drum and bugle corps, a fireworks display, and two searchlights, the Tri-State's staff had to turn away 500 cars after reaching capacity.

Commonwealth ran the Tri-State for all of its life, and there wouldn't be too much to talk about except for the promotion efforts of manager Bob Walter. In 1958, he brought in four Air Force sergeants to see whether any of them could watch the film *No Time for Sergeants* without laughing. In 1963, he gave out 4x5-inch calendars marked with occasional free ticket nights, reasoning, "Everyone puts out calendars but nobody provides one to put up in motor cars, and all our customers drive cars!"

In between, Walter ran one of my favorite promotions, the Bugathon. To promote the "buggy" triple feature of *The Deadly Mantis*, *Them*, and *The Angry Red Planet*, the Tri-State offered cash prizes for the biggest bug and the ugliest bug, which had to be alive but in a jar. An extermination company sprayed all cars when they entered, but only with clear water. Over 50 jarred bugs were entered, the lot was almost full, and the drive-in made a healthy profit on three older movies.

A typical page from the car calendars from Tri-State manager Bob Walter. It included a free show on starred weeknights.

The Tri-State's screen stayed up for decades after the drive-in closed, coming down only recently. The ramps are still covered with cars, now next to a used car dealer.

Intermission:

Autoscopes

Joplin also had another type of drive-in, one of two that popped up near Route 66. Its story began in 1953, when Tom Smith of Urbana MO invented the Autoscope. The idea was simple – instead of building one huge screen facing a field of cars, build a circle of much smaller

Buffalo MO hosted the first full-scale Autoscope, with the central projector showing movies to 125 individual screens. Photo from the June 8, 1959 issue of *Boxoffice*.

screens, one for each car. The execution of that idea was extremely complicated, requiring an elaborate system of mirrors and lenses, but Smith worked it out.

Smith said that his system gave every car a clearer, more equitable picture instead of some on the edges of a wide viewing field trying to watch a large screen at an

Cars got very close to their screens, which were smaller than some home flat-screen televisions today. Photo from the June 8, 1959 issue of *Boxoffice*.

Multi-Screen Drive-In Going Up in Albuquerque

The best opportunity for the Autoscope to succeed was the Circle Autoscope, built in Albuquerque NM in 1963. This was inventor Tom Smith's first (only?) try at a twin-level installation, providing the size, 259 screens, it needed to compete in an urban market. Artist's drawing and headline from the April 8, 1963 issue of *Boxoffice*.

angle. His Autoscopes required less land than conventional drive-ins, and they avoided the expensive construction and maintenance of a huge screen tower. The smaller, translucent screens, each about the size of a 55-inch flat screen TV, were less prone to wind damage and could be easily replaced inexpensively.

The first Autoscope opened in Urbana in July 1953 with 42 screens. The next year, he opened a larger version, 125 screens, in Buffalo MO. In 1960, Smith adapted Buffalo's setup to show widescreen movies, and that's when other operators started to get interested. The Circle Autoscope in Albuquerque opened in 1963, the first of its type near Route 66. That drive-in could have been called the Double Circle; it had two concentric rings of screens, one five feet higher and 50 feet farther from the center. Joplin's Mini Drive-In, a single circle with 118 screens, opened in 1971.

Although he didn't use the word "privacy," that was implied in what Smith told *Boxoffice* about the difference in the viewing experience. "Its individual screens give an 'exclusive' feeling to the patron," he said, "the same personal impact that the individual speakers had when they were introduced." That relatively isolated feeling helped the Mini find its eventual core audience, folks who wanted to watch sexy movies, privately.

This flyer for the Circle's grand opening is the only color photo I've ever seen of any Autoscope in action. It closed three months after it opened.

In those days before the internet or even home video, if a fan of *Marital Fulfillment* or *Captain Lust* wanted to watch that movie, he had to find a theater that was showing it. The Mini's tiny screens prevented neighbors or anyone driving along the road from watching. Albuquerque's Circle never switched to naughty movies, which might explain why it closed three months after it opened. On the other hand, the Mini survived until about 1985, about the time when home VCRs became affordable.

In 1973, a company called U.S. TRAD ran an ad in *Boxoffice* saying that eight Autoscopes had already been built. That matches the total I know about – the four above plus Anchorage AK, Houston TX, Richland WA, and Springdale AR. The ad said that 15 more would open that year, including one in Tulsa, but I don't think any of that happened. The Autoscope was an invention in search of a purpose, and the purpose it found is long gone.

Kansas

If you're a glass half-empty kind of reader, you might sneer at Kansas for having only a single drive-in on Route 66. If you're like me, you celebrate the state for having the highest density of drive-ins for its section of the Mother Road – one every 13 miles. Along with Illinois, Kansas was one of two states with its entire section pre-paved when Route 66 was commissioned in 1926.

Baxter Springs

Baxter Springs is just south of the Rainbow Curve Bridge, the only single-span concrete Marsh arch bridge that survives on Route 66. It was built in 1923 and restored in 1994. You can still drive over, but only one way, and not when Brush Creek floods.

Twilite Drive-In

Opened: June 11, 1953

Closed: Oct. 30, 1977

Capacity: 300 cars

Location: On Route 66 just north of the Oklahoma border.

Louis Stein is one of the few people I've heard of who owned both kinds of drive-ins. In his home town of Parsons KS, he owned both Louie's Drive-In restaurant and the Parsons Drive-In Theatre. In late 1952, Stein built the Cherokee Drive-In in Columbus KS, and the

The skeleton of the base of the Twilite's sign, the "Theatre" part above, still sits along old Route 66. Photo courtesy of the Baxter Springs Heritage Center and Museum.

following spring, he added his third and final drive-in theater 50 miles away on the south side of Baxter Springs.

The Twilite Drive-In used a ranch motif, with plenty of rocks and California redwood. Opening night featured a fireworks display and the film *The Magic Carpet*, which was two years old but starred Lucille Ball, then dominating TV ratings with *I Love Lucy*.

Dickinson Theatres, which at that point owned the 66 and Webb City drive-ins just across the border in Missouri, purchased the Twilite in early 1968. After modernizing the facilities, Dickinson ran the drive-in for the rest of its life, closing the Twilite after the 1977

The Twilite's playground was next to its concession stand. Photo courtesy of the Baxter Springs Heritage Center and Museum.

season. Today, its driveways still adjoin the former Route 66, and the wooden base of its marquee stands between them. The Twilite's ramps are still a vacant field, fenced off from the road.

Intermission:
Common Denominators

Some drive-in elements were so common that they aren't worth mentioning. For example, they all had screens and ticket booths. Similarly, some drive-in stories were so common that I'll just list their categories here.

Young patrons snuck into the drive-in, often in car trunks. In the old days when owners kept most of their ticket money, getting in without paying was taking cash out of their pockets. They hated that.

Dating couples sometimes lost interest in the movie and became more enthusiastic about being with each other. Some of those couples later became parents. I'll leave it at that.

One of the drive-in theater fads, mostly in the 1950s, was miniature trains to complement children's playgrounds. Few of them were as miniature as this one, made by the Sunshine Choo-Choo Co. for the Springfield (MO) Drive-In. Photo from the April 10, 1961 issue of *Boxoffice*.

From their beginnings as accidental profit centers to their eventual, modern cafeteria style, concession stands evolved fast. I'll write more about that in the next intermission.

Burglars targeted drive-in safes, and robbers loved to hold up box offices. A drive-in would build up a lot of cash on weekends, and it was easy for a motorized bandit to drive up, complete his transaction, and zoom off.

In the mid-1950s, almost all pre-existing drive-ins widened their screens to accommodate CinemaScope and other wide film formats.

In those innocent days of reduced litigation, back when childhood injuries were seen as a rite of passage, drive-ins usually provided playgrounds. These weren't today's safety-rated plastic fixtures. We're talking 20-foot slides, long seesaws, and puke-inducing spinners, machined out of heavy-duty steel and bolted onto thick, unforgiving slabs of concrete. Parents probably thought it made their kids tougher.

On Sunday mornings, many drive-ins hosted drive-in religious services. This happened a lot every spring on Easter Sunday.

In the 1960s and later, many drive-ins added weekend flea markets.

There are still more obvious common denominators – concentric ramps to tilt the car to the screen, fencing to prevent cars from bypassing the box office, etc. – but let's keep this intermission short. On to Oklahoma!

The 66 in Carthage MO still has some of its original playground equipment, built to last. 2021 photo by the author.

Oklahoma

Leaving out its pre-1937, pre-drive-in alignment in New Mexico, Route 66's longest stretch in any state is in Oklahoma. It's only fair that it's also the state with the most drive-ins on this list, 29 of them. Oklahoma has tiny small-town drive-ins, huge big-city drive-ins, and everything in between.

Miami

Prepare to be confused. This city isn't in Florida or Ohio, and it should be pronounced My-am-UH instead of My-am-EE. But the really confusing part is the history of its drive-ins' names.

Tri-State / Sooner Drive-In

Opened: June 30, 1949

Closed: 1989

Capacity: 500 cars

Location: On Route 66 north of town by the Miami Airport.

A year after the Tri-State Drive-In in nearby Joplin MO opened to sellout crowds, Griffith Theatres decided to build its own drive-in in Miami and also name it the Tri-State. Griffith soon became Video Independent Theatres, and that's the company that ran it for most of its life.

In March 1955, the Tri-State widened its screen to 46x82 feet, "twice the size as the picture formerly used," according to the *Miami Daily News-Record*. Then in August 1963, things got confusing. As you'll read below, Video's attempt to build a second Miami drive-in was a failure, but its nice neon sign was still just sitting there. Whether to take advantage of that sign or to stop being mistaken for its rival in Joplin, management moved the sign to the Tri-State site and renamed it the Sooner Drive-In.

The Tri-State as it looked in the 1950s. Photo via MiamiHistory.net.

Martin Theatres, later known as Carmike, bought Video's holdings in 1983. The second Miami Sooner apparently closed at the end of the 1989 season. It was definitely finished by February 1991, when drive-in movie critic Joe Bob Briggs wrote, "The folks in Miami, Okla., have just about given up hope that the Sooner Drive-In will ever reopen. The screen has started to rot, casting weird shadows on the Wal-Mart across the highway." That Wal-Mart subsequently moved across the street and occupies the site today.

Sooner Drive-In

Opened: July 2, 1953

Closed: June 19, 1954

Capacity: 300 cars

Location: On Route 66 about 1.5 miles south of town at the intersection with US 59.

Business was so good at Video Independent's Tri-State on the north side of Miami that it soon began construction at the intersection of US 59 and 66 in the Dotyville neighborhood on the south side. When it was finished, the back of its 50-foot screen tower displayed

This sign was so nice that Video Independent Theatres used it twice. Photo posted by Chris1982 at CinemaTreasures.org.

"Sooner" written in neon script letters. The screen on the other side was 36x46 feet.

There was only one, fatal flaw at the Sooner – like much of Miami, it was prone to flooding. After battling the waters in the spring of 1954, management added a note to its June 18th newspaper ad. It warned that due to damage to the driveways and ramps caused by heavy rains, the drive-in would be closed after the 19th for resurfacing of the parking area "and will remain closed until all repairs are complete!" It appears that never happened, though the site still looked intact in a 1958 aerial photo. Video moved the sign to its north-side drive-in in 1963. Today, the former driveway to the original Sooner and its viewing field are covered in trees.

Vinita

Route 66 fans love roadside oddities, but I still feel guilty about loving the huge arched service plaza over I-44 southeast of town. Not only is it on the highway that replaced the Mother Road here, this oasis also intercepts eastbound travelers before reaching Vinita. Opened in 1958 as The Glass House restaurant, it later became the world's largest McDonalds. After a 2014 remodeling, it's now the multi-restaurant Will Rogers Archway.

Undated photo (probably 1961, cropped) by Taylor Studio, Vinita OK. From the William B. Turk Collection, Oklahoma Historical Society via The Gateway to Oklahoma History.

Lariat Drive-In

Opened: June 14, 1950

Closed: 1984?

Capacity: 300 cars

Location: On Route 66 about two miles west of town.

Video Independent Theatres opened the Lariat with an Old West theme in 1950, its letters written in script on the back of its screen tower. Few photos of the drive-in survive, and its lifelong corporate ownership helped keep it quiet and orderly. By 1956, management had attached a wide screen to the screen tower. For Memorial Day Weekend 1958, the Lariat offered an "all-night rock-athon," with *The Girl Can't Help It*; *Love Me Tender*;

Shake, Rattle and Rock!; *Dragstrip Girl*; *Rock All Night*; and *Runaway Daughters*.

Georgia-based Martin Theatres bought Video Independent's theaters in 1983. Martin's list of holdings, published in the 1984 edition of the *Motion Picture Almanac*, included the Lariat. The following year, the Lariat was off Martin's list, suggesting that it closed sometime in 1984. A church occupies the site today.

Claremore

In the 1920s and 30s, Will Rogers was a hugely popular film star and humorist. (He began his lectures by noting, "A humorist entertains, and a lecturer annoys.") Rogers was born in Claremore, the seat of Rogers County, which was named after his father. So much of this town is named after one Rogers or another that it's only right that the drive-in was too.

Rogers Drive-In

Opened: June 16, 1950

Closed: October 1996

Capacity: 296 cars

Location: On State Highway 20 about 2.6 miles east of Route 66.

When Video Independent Theatres opened this drive-in, the 50-foot screen tower featured a neon portrait of Will Rogers with a rope twisting in his hand. How I wish I had a photo of that! The other side of the tower, facing northeast, held the largest screen in the county, 29x39 feet. The drive-in held about 300 cars with a speaker for each.

Carmike absorbed Video in 1983, but Leo Woodall bought the Rogers and owned the drive-in for the rest of its life. Jake Bowden ran the Rogers from 1963 until it closed at the end of the 1996 season. The drive-in was soon razed to be replaced by the storage units that are still there today.

A block of storage units had carved a chunk from the Rogers' viewing area in this 1968 USGS photo.

Tulsa

Cyrus Avery, the father of Route 66, is well recognized in his adopted hometown of Tulsa. The Cyrus Avery Centennial Plaza is on the northeast side of the Arkansas River, nearest downtown, and the other side of the river has a collection of restored neon motel signs. In between is the old Route 66 bridge, now called the Cyrus Avery Memorial Bridge.

Other Tulsa drive-ins more than three miles from Route 66: Sand Springs / Capri (1950-1995), Skyline (1948-1971).

Hi-Way 66 / 11th Street Drive-In

Opened: Aug. 21, 1947

Closed: Sept. 15, 1982

Capacity: 1000 cars

Location: On Route 66 by Mingo Road on the east side of town.

Although it advertised as the Hi-Way 66, the drive-in's screen tower had just a "66 Drive-In" in neon. It also looks like it had some kind of neon mural on the bottom half. 1962 photo (cropped) by Howard Hopkins, Hopkins Photography Company, from the Tulsa Historical Society and Museum.

Griffith Theatres built the first drive-in to be named after the Mother Road, opening it as the "Hi-Way 66". It was also Tulsa's first drive-in, and its single screen faced a lot that could hold about 560 cars. Huge loudspeakers provided the sound when it opened, annoying the neighbors, but Griffith installed in-car speakers the following season. The first time the Hi-Way 66 closed, it was for a couple of months in 1956 because of highway construction. The second time was after the 1959 season, and I'm still not sure why.

Video Independent Theatres, essentially the new name for Griffith, gave the old 66 a fresher start in 1964. The reopened drive-in became the 11th Street, since US 66 had been rerouted. It added a second screen in 1966,

Between 1959, when it closed as the Hi-Way 66, and 1964, when it reopened as the 11th Street, the drive-in's sign deteriorated. 1962 photo (cropped) by Howard Hopkins, Hopkins Photography Company, from the Tulsa Historical Society and Museum.

almost doubling its capacity to 1000 cars. A flood hit the drive-in in 1976, filling the concession stand with three feet of water. Video cleaned up the mess, and the 11th Street continued until closing after the 1982 season. A church and a storage facility occupy the site today.

Airview Drive-In

Opened: June 7, 1951

Closed: Sept. 10, 1981

Capacity: 700 cars

Location: On Pine Street due south of Tulsa Municipal Airport, about two miles north of Route 66.

A sure sign that the drive-in was near an airport, besides the airplane on the side of the screen tower, was its name "Airview" painted on the roof. Photo by M. H. Millard, Sky Signs Aerial Advertising, from the Tulsa Historical Society and Museum.

Video Independent Theatres added another drive-in to its portfolio in 1951, naming it for its view of the airport. Its most notable feature was its free, elaborate children's playground. "Storybook Lane" included a miniature train, car rides, a merry-go-round, the usual swings and slides, and something called a "giant ocean wave." The Airview's second-most notable feature was its airplane theme, with a 30-foot jet plane on the back of its screen tower and a neon-outlined plane on its marquee.

The Airview lived a quiet, corporate-owned existence, owned by Video for all of its life. It closed after the 1981 season. The Laura Dester Shelter for children occupies the site today.

When the Admiral Twin rebuilt its double-sided screen after the disastrous fire of 2010, it used metal supports instead of wood. Good choice! The drive-in requires two full-sized projection-concession stands, one for each side of the viewing field. 2019 photo by the author.

Modernaire / Admiral Twin Drive-In

Opened: May 24, 1951

~~Closed:~~ active

Capacity: 1350 cars

Location: This one's a little tricky. A roadside attraction sign at the Admiral Twin says that it was once on Route 66, but that's not strictly accurate. The original alignment of US 66 was there, but in July 1932, long before the Modernaire existed, the highway moved to 11th Street. When the drive-in was built, it connected to US 75, a mile north of the Mother Road.

Over its 70 years, this drive-in has seen a lot. To start, L. E. (Earl) Snyder built the Modernaire as his second drive-in, after the Apache. The Modernaire's single screen faced west. Before the year was out, Snyder sold the drive-in to Henry Robb of Dallas.

Robb took a local partner, Harry Hardgrave, for the 1952 season, and in June, they renamed the drive-in the Admiral after the local street name for US 75. In November 1952, Hardgrave was charged with showing a "lewd" film, as the assistant county attorney claimed indecent pictures were spliced into *Bob and Sally*. In October 1953, Hardgrave died of a heart attack.

Two months after Hardgrave passed away, Alex Blue of McAlester OK bought in as a partner and manager of the Admiral. In 1955, Blue announced that the drive-in would become the first in the state with a double-sided screen, enlarged to 92x50 feet. This required two projection rooms, and in the beginning, two snack bars. This also doubled the drive-in's capacity, from 675 to 1350 cars. The renamed Admiral Twin at first used the two screens for the same movie with staggered start times, but soon switched to different movies.

In 1966, General Cinema Corp. bought the Admiral Twin from Robb and Blue. The next few decades were quiet, except when Frances Ford Coppola used it as a location for his 1983 film *The Outsiders*. Around 1987, GCC, run by Richard A. Smith, sold the Admiral Twin, by then its last drive-in, to Richard D. Smith. The second Smith managed the drive-in for the next dozen years; his son Blake officially took over in 2000.

In 2005, Hampton Hotels' "Save-A-Landmark" program provided 100 hours of labor and 50 gallons of paint to spruce up the Admiral Twin. Then in September 2010, a fire destroyed the double-sided screen tower. With community support, the Smiths put together enough funds to rebuild the tower, using metal this time, and reopened in June 2012. The Admiral Twin celebrated its 70th anniversary in 2021.

The base of the marquee in front of the screen tower is still there today. Undated photo from the Tulsa Historical Society and Museum.

Apache Drive-In

Opened: July 7, 1948

Closed: 1979

Capacity: 225 cars

Location: On Apache Street just east of Harvard Avenue, three miles north of Route 66.

After doing his part in the armed forces in World War II, former theater usher Earl Snyder believed that drive-in theaters were about to hit it big so he built some of his own. His first effort was the Apache, designed for an African-American audience in then-segregated Tulsa. When the drive-in opened, the *Oklahoma Eagle* wrote that it "offers to mothers, sisters and the entire family a chance to see the full picture with no baby problem and no parking problems for father."

At some point, the Apache integrated its audience. I'm not sure when that was, but it might have been just two weeks after it opened. On July 23, 1948, the *Tulsa World* ran an ad for the "New Apache," which said it was "A Family Theater for all Tulsa."

Was this 1948 *Tulsa World* ad a signal that the Apache had integrated?

The times kept changing. Tulsa became less segregated in the mid-1950s, and Snyder's company became Family Theatres. According to the *Motion Picture Almanac*, Family continued to own the Apache for the rest of its life. A photo caption in *Tulsa Movie Theaters*, co-authored by the Tulsa Historical Society, said the Apache closed in 1979. Today, the rusted base of the Apache's old marquee is still visible in a grassy field across the street from the northeast campus of Tulsa Community College.

Sheridan Drive-In

Opened: April 20, 1951

Closed: 1963

Capacity: 650 cars

Location: On Sheridan Road north of 51st Street, across the street from Brown Airport. That put it less than a mile away from US 66 when it was routed along I-44 in 1960.

The Sheridan's screen tower had a modern look with a neon shooting star at the top. 1962 photo by Howard Hopkins, Hopkins Photography Company, from the Tulsa Historical Society and Museum.

Video Independent Theatres owned dozens of indoor theaters in Oklahoma but only a few drive-ins when it built the Sheridan across the street from Brown Airport. Its elaborate Cartoonville playground, "a real amusement park all for free," included a miniature train, merry-go-round, swings, slides, and more. Its screen tower was about as tall as the airport's control tower less than half a mile away.

The Sheridan was owned by Video for all of its short life, making for a quiet existence. By 1955, Video widened its screen. Both the drive-in and Brown Airport were intact in 1962, but were long gone by 1967, when housing developments had overrun the formerly pastoral area. No trace of the Sheridan or the small airport survives today.

The Riverside's screen tower was patched above the "iv," where winds had punched a hole. 1962 photo by Howard Hopkins, Hopkins Photography Company, from the Tulsa Historical Society and Museum.

Riverside Drive-In

Opened: May 7, 1948

Closed: Nov. 30, 1977

Capacity: 602 cars

Location: On 71st Street a half mile east of the Arkansas River, about two miles south of Route 66.

When Griffith Theatres opened the Riverside, it was Tulsa's third drive-in. Griffith became Video Independent Theatres, and that's who owned it for the rest of its 30 seasons. Today it's completely gone, replaced by an apartment complex.

The best story I could find about the Riverside concerned two of its employees. Not so long after it opened, a young pilot attending the nearby Spartan School of Aeronautics got a job at the Riverside. Donald Sloan reportedly "ran the spotlights" while Mary Stunkard worked the ticket booth. Sloan proposed, and the two of them were married for 56 years before he passed away in 2006.

One more thing. In the 1980s, Tulsa's historic White House Mansion was rescued from demolition and moved in pieces from Cherry Street near downtown to a pastoral setting about a mile south of the old drive-in site. The mansion's renovated ballroom floor is made of wood from a former bowling alley, and its support beams came from pieces of the Riverside.

Bellaire Drive-In

Opened: June 5, 1953

Closed: 1979

Capacity: 600 cars

Location: Just west of the I-44/US 66 bridge over the Arkansas River.

Earl Snyder had a nice run as the head of Family Theatres. First he built Tulsa's Apache Drive-In, then the Modernaire, which he sold the same year it opened. In 1954, a year after he opened the Bellaire, Snyder helped convince the city to stay away from Daylight Saving Time. He bought the Capri Drive-In in 1963, and two years later, his Boman Twin was just the third indoor two-screen theater in the US.

I'm a little surprised the Bellaire survived so long even though it was practically across the highway from a wastewater treatment plant. Southern breezes carried a stinky smell to the viewing field. The drive-in employed only married women in its concession stand and married men in other full-time jobs. In the 1950s, attendants would take concession orders from customers who didn't want to leave their cars.

After Snyder died in 1967, his wife Marjorie continued to operate and expand the local business, though she closed the Bellaire after the 1979 season. Car dealerships occupy the site today.

The Bellaire was just north of the highway. 1967 photo © HistoricAerials.com, used by permission.

Sapulpa

This city was named for the Native American who established a trading post at Polecat and Rock creeks. Sapulpa later became the county seat of Creek County. This is also where you'll find the Heart of Route 66 Auto Museum, which commissioned the world's largest gas pump next door.

Tee-Pee Drive-In

Opened: May 5, 1950

Closed: 1999

Capacity: 400 cars

Location: On Ozark Trail just across the Rock Creek Bridge from Route 66 west of town.

Griffith Theatres announced that it purchased the land for Sapulpa's drive-in in November 1949, and one month later, the company became Video Independent Theaters. In early 1950, Video ran a naming contest won by Mrs. B. F. Wooden, Jr., who suggested the Tee-Pee. (Through the years, that name was sometimes spelled as two words or as one unhyphenated word, but I'll keep the original here.)

The Tee-Pee's viewing field was 6½ acres, made into a hard surface with a coating of "Dustrol." Speakers were available for 350 cars, with room to expand to 500 cars. Fireworks and a floodlight attracted a capacity crowd on opening night. Except for replacing a storm-damaged screen in May 1960, its first three decades were fairly quiet.

In the 1980s, the Tee-Pee's life got turbulent. The drive-in apparently took 1982 off; its first newspaper ad that year appeared on Sept. 27th, when the Tee-Pee

Between the Tee-Pee (screen visible in the background) and the rest of Sapulpa is the Rock Creek Bridge, built in 1924, now closed. Circa 2016 photo © 4kclips / DepositPhotos.com.

A promoter persuaded locals to clean up the Tee-Pee's grounds in 2012. By 2019, when the author took this picture, nature had begun reclaiming the screen.

announced it was for sale. Later that year, a sandblasting company asked the city to rezone the "vacant" drive-in for industrial use but was turned down. Then on March 17, 1983, the Tee-Pee ran a "Gala Re-opening" ad.

The following year, on May 3, 1984, the Tee-Pee's newspaper ad said that it was under new ownership. That lines up with a change in its *Motion Picture Almanac* listing, now showing J. Malone in charge. This time the drive-in continued advertising through 1993, then went quiet again.

Marsha Baccus and her husband bought a half-interest in the Tee-Pee in 1993, but couldn't get the other half until 1996. They started renovating the drive-in in 1997, using a previously installed FM radio system for the sound and re-wiring 300 speakers. The drive-in reopened in August that year and stayed active through the 1999 season before closing yet again.

There was a weird episode in 2012. A promoter with a self-described track record of drive-in restoration came to town and persuaded some folks to clear the overgrown brush off the viewing area. After digging into his past, some of the locals became skeptical of the promoter's stories. He quickly left the picture.

The Kante Group, headed by Joni Rogers-Kante, bought the Tee-Pee in March 2021 and immediately began clearing the site to begin renovations. Rogers-Kante said that the new drive-in could include vintage, immobile cars and recreational vehicles for rent "for those who don't have a car." Plans call for the Tee-Pee to reopen in the spring of 2022.

Bristow

Bristow began as a small trading post, then expanded when the future Frisco Railroad built a stop there. Future movie star Gene Autry worked as a telegraph operator at the train depot, since remade as the Bristow Historical Museum.

Pirate Drive-In

Opened: June 28, 1953

Closed: 1981?

Capacity: 220 cars

Location: On Route 66, about 1.5 miles west of town.

Harry Walling, who operated a couple of indoor theaters in Bristow, announced in May 1950 that he had staked out a spot for a new drive-in. Two months later, Henry Simpson led a group that took over Walling's little theater chain, and the drive-in plans were left on the shelf.

In 1953, Simpson dusted off those plans and began building the Pirate west of town. Workers rushed to take advantage of the summer season even as they waited for the arrival of sound equipment. In the end, the timing was so uncertain that the Pirate's grand opening had no advance notice except a sound truck announcement the night before.

The Pirate was small; capacity estimates over the years ranged from 200 to 300. Perhaps that's why its owners always needed a side gig. Simpson split his time between movie work and as Creek County deputy sheriff. He resigned as deputy in 1960 to spend more time on his theaters, then rejoined as deputy sheriff again in 1963.

The top of a typical 1957 ad for the Pirate in the *Bristow News*.

In early 1963, Simpson's mother-in-law, Willie Wilkinson, passed away from carbon monoxide caused by a faulty gas heater. She was part-owner of Bristow's theaters, and her son Bill Wilkinson bought out Simpson's share. The younger Wilkinson soon split his time between running the Pirate and attending the University of Oklahoma.

In 1969, Freeman Holmes and O. D. Holt bought the Pirate. They upgraded the equipment in the projection booth in 1973. Holmes had a mobile home business on the side, and he sold the drive-in in 1974 to devote more time to that enterprise. Richard Stromme became the Pirate's last owner. The drive-in was still intact in 1980, but closed soon after. A small cluster of storage buildings occupies the site today.

Davenport

The area that would become Davenport was homesteaded by Noah and Annie Sutton Davenport in the Land Run of 1891. The town incorporated in 1906 and paved its main street with bricks in 1926. That street, Broadway, is listed in the National Register of Historic Places.

Rig Drive-In

Opened: July 1953

Closed: August 1962

Capacity: 200 cars

Location: On Route 66 a mile northeast of town.

Joe Stribling was a manager for the Griffith / Video Independent theater chain before moving to Davenport in the early 1950s. He and his wife bought the indoor Gem Theater there. In 1953, they built the Rig, named for the area's oil derricks. On the side, Joe worked for the telephone company, and the wife taught piano lessons.

After 10 seasons with two theaters, Davenport lost them

Detail of a matchbook cover posted by ScreenTower at CinemaTreasures.

This was part of a series of pictures of Davenport businesses, all taken to be mailed to a US Army serviceman in Korea so he would feel less homesick. Photo circa 1953 from the Jones family collection.

both in 1962. Stribling announced that summer that he was dismantling the Rig and storing its equipment at the Gem until he could sell it. With their primary jobs taking most of their time, they said they couldn't properly show movies too. *Boxoffice* wrote, "That and a decline in business caused them to call it quits." The Rig's old viewing field is now an empty lot south of old Route 66.

Edmond

Route 66 made a sharp left turn in downtown Edmond, heading towards the state capitol building. The city is home to the first public school house in the Oklahoma Territory, and to the *Edmond Sun*, which was the state's oldest continuously published newspaper until 2020, when it merged with the *Norman Transcript*.

Woodstock / Edmond Drive-In

Opened: Sept 20, 1971

Closed: 1980?

Capacity: 200 cars

Location: On North Boulevard, about 1.4 miles north of Routh 66 just before it turned south.

The Woodstock had a brief life, but it was rarely dull. It started with Ron Turner, who owned the Sunset Drive-In in Muskogee. Turner built the Woodstock in the summer of 1971, barely opening before cold weather set in that year. He had partnered with James O'Donnell two years later when they decided to stage a rock music festival on the grounds. (No, it wasn't *that* Woodstock.) A young girl was injured during the show, and a judge awarded her damages in 1974.

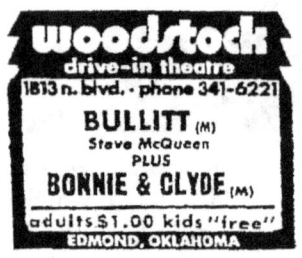

A typical 1972 Woodstock ad in the *Daily Oklahoman*.

In 1976, Edward Roupe bought the Woodstock from Turner and O'Donnell. Roupe ran it for just one season. In 1977, James Barnet leased it from him and advertised it in the *Daily Oklahoman* as the Edmond Drive-In. Those were the final newspaper ads for any drive-in in Edmond. In 1980, the drive-in returned to the local phone book after an absence of three years, and the *Motion Picture Almanac* mentioned it for the first time, still owned by Roupe. It was intact in a 1981 aerial photo, but that's the only evidence that it operated in the 80s. Today, Graceland Cemetery to the south is expanding into the old Woodstock site.

Sundown Drive-In

Opened: July 3, 1951

Closed: September 1955?

Capacity: 300 cars

Location: On Route 66 a few blocks south of 15th Street.

Brothers Jack and Jimmy Hull built their drive-in theater in 1951, when the Defense Production Act, passed at the start of the Korean War, still hampered the use of some materials needed to build entertainment venues. (Indeed, the National Production Authority turned down a request by C. H. Spearman and Hazel McCoy to build another Edmond drive-in later that year.) The result for the Hulls was barely enough to open the Sundown. It started with a 46-foot screen but no playground or marquee board – those would be added when the NPA allowed.

Somehow, by the end of the 1952 season, M. A. Harris became the owner of the Sundown. Other information about the drive-in is sparse until Aug. 28, 1955, when a strong windstorm damaged the screen. Workers quickly tried to make repairs that week so the Sundown's normal

The top of a typical 1952 Sundown ad in the *Oklahoma County Register*.

schedule could continue. Then on Sept. 29, "hurricane-force" winds knocked down a highway patrol radio tower and destroyed the Sundown's screen and concession stand. There's no evidence that the drive-in was ever rebuilt. A Home Depot occupies the site today.

Oklahoma City

Thanks to its huge acreage, large population, and favorable latitude, Oklahoma City had 11 drive-ins in simultaneous operation in 1967. There aren't many cities that can top that. But because Route 66 and its bypasses and alternates stayed on the north side of town, only seven of those drive-ins were close enough for this list.

Other Oklahoma City drive-ins more than three miles from Route 66: 14 Flags (1968-1982), Airline (1950-1973), Hillcrest (1964-1992), Odom / 77 (1947-1975), Riviera (1967-1999), Skyview (1948-1983), Winchester (1968-present).

N'eastern 66 / 66 / Cinema 66 Drive-In

Opened: August 4, 1950

Closed: May 31, 1968

Capacity: 600 cars

Location: About a quarter-mile south of Route 66 on Grand Boulevard.

In 1949, Leo and Lydia Thomas came to Oklahoma City, where they designed and built this drive-in on what they called a natural amphitheater. They ran it together for the next 11 years, though early on, they formed some kind of partnership or operating agreement with the local

Barton theater chain, which was listed as the drive-in's owner in 1951. In the late 1950s, the Thomases added the NE Bowling Center nearby.

The N.Eastern's second *Daily Oklahoman* ad still included directions via the "New 66 cut-off."

The drive-in bounced around with a bunch of names. The *Motion Picture Almanac* showed it as the "N. Eastern Drive-In." In newspapers, the drive-in advertised at first as the "N.Eastern 66" or the "N.E. 66." That changed to simply 66 in 1962, then to the Cinema 66 in 1964. The Barton chain was sold in June 1968 to Ferris Enterprises, which immediately closed the Cinema 66. The drive-in's ad in the *Daily Oklahoman* on June 8, 1969 said that it was closed for remodeling, and to "Watch for re-opening later this summer!" That never happened. Trees have reclaimed the old NE 66 site, now immediately south of a large indoor multiplex cinema.

Fair Park Drive-In

Opened: July 17, 1948

Closed: August 18, 1948?

Capacity: 250 cars

Location: At 10th Street and Bryant Avenue, about 2.6 miles east-southeast of Route 66 at the State Capitol Building.

Very little information survives about the short-lived Fair Park. It was built by Southwestern Theaters Co., headed by Horace Falls, at a cost of $50,000. Its screen faced southeast. The *Daily Oklahoman* noted its opening by calling it "the first drive-in theater in the southwest" for African-Americans, overlooking Tulsa's Apache, which had opened earlier that month.

The Fair Park's grand opening ad in the *Black Dispatch* mentioned that it had a concession stand and seats for walk-in patrons. Two weeks later, its ad featured a free weekday ticket and the promise of giveaways on Saturdays. The Fair Park's final ad on Aug. 14 included its slate of movies through the 18th. And then nothing. In the drive-in's only industry directory appearance, the 1948-49 *Theatre Catalog* listed it with a capacity of 250 cars. Falls moved to Dallas in 1949. A 1954 aerial photo showed only the remnants of arced ramps in the former viewing field.

Oklahoma historian Wesley Horton once wrote, "Sewage treatment plants killed two drive-in theatres

Tulsa's Apache Drive-In had opened two weeks before this ad in the *Black Dispatch*, so the Fair Park wasn't really the only OK African American drive-in.

in OKC, the Fairpark Drive-In and the North Penn Twin Drive-In." The Fair Park was less than a half mile northeast of a sewage disposal facility. Today the drive-in site is a wooded area at the northeast corner of Douglass Park. The sewage plant, now a covered "water pollution control facility," is on the south side of the park.

Northwest Highway Drive-In

Opened: July 2, 1947

Closed: Sept. 15, 1979

Capacity: 756 cars

Location: On the Northwest Highway (of course), AKA State Highway 3, at Independence Avenue, about 1.2 miles north of Route 66.

Odom Farrell Sullivan was a longtime theater man in Wichita KS, and was even mayor there for a few months. In 1947, he partnered with another guy from Wichita, R. E. Conrad, to build a drive-in in Oklahoma City.

The Northwest Highway, abbreviated "NW. Hi-Way" on its screen tower, tied for the first drive-in in Oklahoma City. It opened on the same night as the Odom, (too far south for this list), which was started by Peerless Theaters and

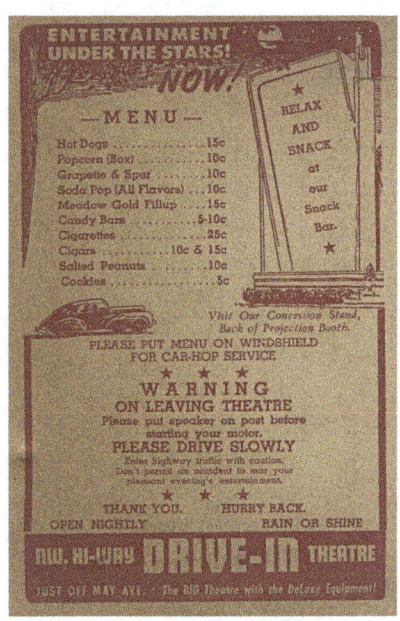

Spur Cola was first sold in 1948, which is one clue to the date of this menu.

completed by the R. Lewis Barton chain. Peerless was a Wichita company, so the drive-in might have been named for Sullivan. Barton changed the Odom's name the following spring to the 77 Drive-In. But I digress.

Sullivan Theatres sold the Northwest Highway to Barton Theatres in the summer of 1952. Barton ran the drive-in the longest, until 1968, when Mississippi-based Gulf States Theatres took over all of Barton's Oklahoma City drive-ins. By 1973, Gulf States had closed them all. In June 1974, Burke Enterprises bought the Northwest Highway, along with the Sooner Twin and North Penn Twin, and soon advertised them under the Galaxy Theatres banner. George Caporal and Caporal Theatres, which ran the Riviera, bought the Northwest Highway in 1975. Caporal ran the drive-in for the rest of its life, which concluded at the end of the 1979 season. A hotel occupies the site today.

Completed in 1964, the 275-foot Founders Tower overlooked the Northwest Highway. 1969 photo © HistoricAerials.com, used by permission.

North Penn Twin Drive-In

Opened: May 22, 1963

Closed: September 1974

Capacity: 1850 cars

Location: At 122th Street and Pennsylvania Avenue, 2.9 miles west of Route 66 (Kelley Avenue).

In 1961, Barton Theatres bought the site for this drive-in, chasing after the suburbanites who were moving to northern Oklahoma City. When the North Penn Twin open in the spring of 1963, newspaper ads called it the "world's largest" million dollar theater. After buying their tickets, drivers would pass through a tunnel entrance at the base of the screen tower on their way to view either the "Kim" (north) or "Roger" (south) side of the screen.

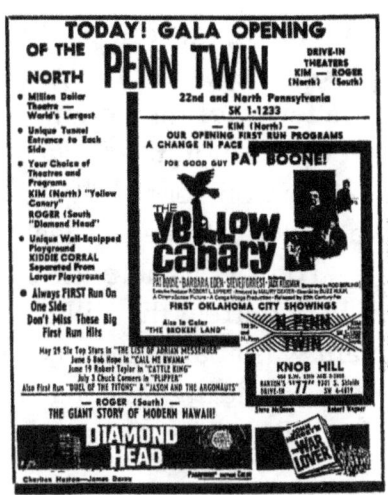

I wonder who the North Penn Twin's screens "Kim" and "Roger" were named after. They first appeared in this *Daily Oklahoman* grand opening ad.

But the North Penn Twin, like the Fair Park before it, had a fatal problem. It was practically adjacent to the sewage treatment plant for The Village, a small nearby city. More suburbanites had moved to the Village, and the heavier load led to the plant requiring frequent repairs. Patrons would call ahead to learn the scent du jour before driving out for a movie.

Barton sued the city in 1964 for lost business caused by the odors that hung over the drive-in for "various unpredictable lengths of time." The Village moved to improve the plant to increase capacity, but the problem and the lawsuit dragged on. In late 1969, the Oklahoma Supreme Court overturned a lower court's ruling and sided with the Bartons, but they had already relinquished control of the North Penn Twin.

In 1968, Mississippi-based Gulf States Theatres took over all of Barton's Oklahoma City drive-ins, occasionally advertising this one as the New Penn Twin. In June 1974, Burke Enterprises bought the drive-in, and operated it for a few months under the Galaxy Theatres banner. The last mention in the *Daily Oklahoman* was a movie roundup on Sept. 8, 1974; it's unclear exactly which night was the North Penn's last show.

Too late to help the drive-in, Oklahoma City agreed in 1979 to treat the Village's sewage. The old disposal plant was abandoned and later replaced by a public works building. An apartment complex occupies the North Penn Twin site today.

Twilight Gardens Drive-In

Opened: Sept. 29, 1950

Closed: Sept. 5, 1972

Capacity: 700 cars

Location: On May Avenue a couple of blocks north of Britton Road, which was a US 66 Alternate when the drive-in opened.

The Twilight Gardens was unusual for Oklahoma City in several respects. It was the only OKC drive-in built by Video Independent Theatres, which owned quite a few of them in the state. Video owned the drive-in for all of its decades of life. And its entryway was remarkably beautiful.

The showpiece of the Twilight Gardens was its color-changing fountain, positioned in a "mirror pool" between Britton Road and the box office. Families who made it into the drive-in could take advantage of "Cartoonville," an elaborate playground with a miniature train, pony rides, all the usual equipment, and the house of the "Old Woman in the Shoe." Benches and seats in

Smaller signs next to the main "Twi-Light" sign advertised the drive-in's Cartoonville playground. 1954 photo from the Z.P. Meyers/Barney Hillerman Photographic Collection of the Oklahoma Historical Society.

front of the concession stand let patrons watch the movie outside their cars.

Although it closed for its first few winters, the Twilight Gardens soon added in-car heaters to stay open year-round except for the very worst storms. That came to an end in 1972, when developers planned to build a shopping center on the site. Although its structures and screen tower were quickly dismantled, the land sat idle until 1981, when developers erected a small office building. The building is still there, on the southwest corner of the lot, and the rest of the old viewing field is now a strip mall.

The opening ad for the Twilight Gardens in the *Daily Oklahoman* gave a hint of the beauty of its color-changing fountain.

Cinema 70 Drive-In

Opened: June 19, 1964

Closed: September 1981

Capacity: 1400 cars

Location: On the Northwest Expressway, about 2.3 miles north of Route 66.

Father and son Charles and Maurice Ferris designed this drive-in to use 70mm projectors, but they ran a public naming contest for it in early 1964. I wonder if anyone submitted "Cinema 70" as an entry, or whether they had that idea themselves. When the drive-in opened, its long, narrow viewing field faced a 55x124-foot, all-steel screen tower. It also boasted a 40x70-foot concession stand, with a breezeway patio, and a playground with attendants.

In 1968, ownership started getting turbulent. Ferris Enterprises re-branded itself as Spectro that February. In June, Gulf States Theatres combined Spectro's holdings with the old Barton Theatres drive-ins and advertised them under Gulf States for a while. The drive-in went dark in 1973, then Maurice Ferris bought it back that November.

Charles and Maurice Ferris built the Cinema 70 with a very long, very narrow viewing field. 1969 photo © HistoricAerials.com, used by permission.

Farris Shanbour and Oklahoma Cinema Theatres leased the Cinema 70 in early 1974. They remodeled and reopened the drive-in on May 29. The Shanbour company soon changed its name to Heritage Theatres, and the Cinema 70 seemed to be doing well again. However, the drive-in didn't own its land, which its landlord sold after the 1981 season. A shopping center occupies the site today.

Circle / Cinema C Drive-In

Opened: April 2, 1950

Closed: October 1967

Capacity: 500 cars

Location: On 10th Street, just east of the North Canadian River, about 2.4 miles south of Route 66.

Harry Circle, who also owned a couple of Circle Grocery stores, built the drive-in that would bear his name for 15 years. But when? There are hints that the Circle may have opened briefly in 1949, but the date we know for certain was the start of the 1950 season. By 1952, former school teacher W. J. Nethery owned the Circle, and the Barton Theatres chain purchased it in the summer of 1954.

An 80-mile-per-hour wind blew down the screen tower in April 1955. Barton took the occasion to replace it with a wide screen, reopening

The Circle kept it simple in this small ad in the *Daily Oklahoman*. Was this the grand opening or just a season opener?

in May. The drive-in lasted for another decade until Barton closed the Circle in August 1965.

Almost two years later, in July 1967, Greater Oklahoma City Amusements, made up of several former Barton theaters, briefly reopened the Circle as the "Cinema C." The new name was to build a theme with the company's Cinema 66, which it had renamed a few years earlier. In any event, the experiment failed, and the drive-in closed for good at the end of the 1967 season. Storage units and houses occupy the site today.

Bethany

As its biblical name implies, Bethany was founded by Nazarenes as a place where they could worship freely and pass laws against swearing, dancing, and using tobacco. The city includes Wiley Post Airport, which started as the Tulakes Airport. It's not the same Wiley Post Airport that was across May Avenue from the Twilight Gardens when it was built. That one closed in 1955.

Lake Air Drive-In

Opened: April 18, 1950

Closed: Dec. 30, 1967

Capacity: 600 cars

Location: On Route 66 just east of the bridge over the North Canadian River, aka Lake Overholser.

It's not fair that all we care about Charles B. McFarland is that he built the Lake Air Drive-In and ran it for its first eight seasons. The guy graduated valedictorian of his high school class at age 15, then graduated from Notre Dame *cum laude*. After World War II, he

The Lake Air / Lakeside sign frame was still hanging in there in May 2019 when the author took this photo. Less than two years later, it was gone.

helped his mother with her nursery (plants, not kids) while studying at night for his law degree. He and his brother Robert owned the indoor Coronado Theatre, and the year after he was admitted to the bar, they opened the Lake Air.

The drive-in site had been the Lakeside Golf Course before the McFarlands started working on it, probably in 1949. The Lake Air was a first-class operation, with a fully hard-topped viewing field, in-car speakers, the "most beautiful fountain room," and what was then the largest screen around Oklahoma City. Its playground would grow to include a trolley car on tracks, the usual swings and merry-go-round, and a hay barn.

In June 1951, a tornado ripped up the screen and pulled the roof off the projection building, which was in the back of the lot. Two months later, another windstorm knocked over several nearby trees. Highway construction in the middle of the decade added a stronger bridge over the river but cut into the Lake Air's entrance road. By

1958, the McFarlands were advertising that the construction was over, and the drive-in's enclosed balcony and patio seating welcomed patrons again.

In 1959, Barton Theatres added the Lake Air to its roster of Oklahoma City-area drive-in theaters. Barton, later morphing into Greater Oklahoma City Amusements, operated it through the 1967 season. In 1968, the Lake Air was part of the package of theaters absorbed by Gulf States Theatres, but it never reopened. The site later became a go-cart track and a golf range before being completely abandoned around 2003. A perimeter of trees protects the site today, and only its driveway and a chain-link fence remain.

El Reno

El Reno was founded soon after the 1889 land rush and was named after nearby Fort Reno, which was named after Civil War General Jesse Reno. My favorite Route 66 feature in town is the former pedestrian underpass built in 1936 between Cooney and Jenkins streets by a Works Project Administration crew to protect elementary school children.

El Reno / Squaw Drive-In

Opened: Sept. 11, 1948

Closed: 1984?

Capacity: 220 cars

Location: One block north of Route 66 about a half-mile west of town.

In 1948, Blanche Gibson from Cherokee OK owned the indoor Max Theater there. Walter Shuttee, also from

In 2014, local artist Rick Sinnett painted a mural featuring the Oklahoma state bird, the scissor-tailed flycatcher, on the back of El Reno's drive-in screen tower. The mural had become a bit weathered by 2019, when the author took this photo.

Cherokee, was working as the executive vice president for the Citizens National Bank of El Reno. Possibly too busy with the bank, Shuttee brought Gibson to town to supervise construction and operate the El Reno Drive-In.

E. R. "Red" Slocum and Griffith Theatres, which owned El Reno's three indoor houses, announced on Sept. 2 that they had bought their own drive-in site southeast of town. Nothing ever really came of that, but it's likely they didn't like the competition.

The El Reno Drive-In opened to picketing by the projectionists union. Gibson ran an ad complaining that no other theater in town had a union contract, so she was being unfairly singled out. In a lawsuit to stop picketing in front of his bank, Shuttee said that he had sold his share of the drive-in to Gibson. The resolution came in early October when Gibson signed a contract with the union.

In 1949, Gibson installed in-car speakers, shifting away from a central speaker system, and moved the concession stand from the front office to the projection building, advertising that the innovation made it "faster and easier to enter the theater grounds". Had they been selling popcorn at the box office?

Gibson's name faded from the story at this point, and Shuttee was mentioned in industry publications as the owner of the drive-in.

The El Reno's first large ad in the *El Reno Daily Tribune* described many of the drive-in's features.

In February 1952, Shuttee sold the El Reno to a Chickasha theater owner, Opal Gray. Before the 1952 season opener, Gray planted roses and evergreens, and she installed street lights on the road from the highway. Unfortunately, she also renamed the drive-in the Squaw.

(At the time, one of El Reno High School's long-standing pep clubs was called the Squaws. Except for the drive-in's association with two female owners, a rarity at the time, I don't know why else Gray shifted to that word, which was commonly used back then but is now considered an ethnic slur. The former El Reno is the only drive-in to ever take that name.)

Gray kept the Squaw for only a year, selling in March 1953 to Video Independent Theatres, the successor to Griffith. That company, and Slocum in particular, looked out after the drive-in. He passed away in 1965, and Video took full control until Martin Theatres bought the whole company in early 1983.

When did the Squaw close? Martin Theatres listed it in its company holdings in the 1984 and 1985 editions of the *Motion Picture Almanac*. By the 1986 edition, when Martin completed its name change to Carmike, the Squaw was no longer included. A 1995 aerial photo showed that farmland had reclaimed the viewing field. In 2014, Rick Sinnett painted a scissor-tailed flycatcher mural on the back of the old screen tower, which is still standing today.

Weatherford

The saying goes, "If you want to put yourself on the map, print your own map." One corollary could be, if you want to be remembered, run the post office. Lorinda Weatherford ran the town's post office from her homestead, and that's that. Today there's a 122-foot wind turbine blade resting in a park across from Weatherford's city hall, in case you ever wanted to see one up close.

40 West / 66 West Twin Drive-In

Opened: January 1967

Closed: 2007?

Capacity: 385 cars

Location: About a mile and a half west of town on the outer road of I-40/US 66.

Woodie Sylvester worked for Griffith Theatres and Video Independent Theatres, its successor, from 1935 to 1965, taking a break only to help win World War II. He was elected president of the United Theater Owners of

If it had stayed alive, Weatherford's 66 West Drive-In might have become almost as iconic as Carthage MO's 66. Circa 2008 photo © Brad Remy | Dreamstime.com

Oklahoma in March 1965, and that fall, he left Video to buy the Tech Theatre in Weatherford. The following summer, he started work on an all-weather drive-in that would have a 50x70-foot screen and a 30x60-foot projection/concession building.

In July 1966, Sylvester was hoping to open in September. By the end of the year, he was hoping for Dec. 31. I don't think he made it. The first announcement I could find was in the Jan. 18, 1967 *Motion Picture Exhibitor*, followed by a mention in *Boxoffice* in February. Within a few years, son-in-law Doug Hale was helping to run the 40 West.

Sylvester retired in 1980, selling the 40 West and his other Weatherford theaters to the Dan Wolfenbarger chain. Wolfenbarger added a second screen and renamed it the 66 West Twin. Later accounts said that during the

The original screen of the 40 West/66 West lasted the longest. Circa 2010 photo © Harris Shiffman | Dreamstime.com

oil and gas boom of the early 1980s, cars lined the highway every night waiting to get in. But most booms end in a bust, and the 66 West Twin closed in 1984. Dickinson Theatres later built an indoor three-screen theater adjacent to the lot.

The triplex's manager, Brian Gayle, was sufficiently intrigued by the abandoned drive-in that he was able to convince Dickinson to buy it. The 66 Twin reopened in May 1999, having switched away from in-car speakers to radio sound. But it probably wasn't too profitable, since Robert George bought the drive-in and its adjacent indoor theater at a sheriff's sale in 2000.

George, who was running over a dozen theaters in the area, really just wanted the triplex, but he fell in love with the 66 Twin, which he reopened. In 2003, he told the *Daily Oklahoman*, "Even if I had to sell my other theaters, I'd keep my drive-in." But in 2006, George made national news when he offered the drive-in, and the local indoor theaters, on eBay for $195,000.

I'm not sure what happened after that. It appears that the 66 Twin stayed open into the 2007 season, but later that year George ran into some personal issues that might have kept him away from the drive-in. By 2009, the north screen had been removed, and the rest of the drive-in was demolished in 2011. The indoor theater, now a fourplex, is still operating today.

Clinton

Clinton is home to the Oklahoma Route 66 Museum, part of the Oklahoma Historical Society and the first official state-operated Route 66 museum. Clinton also has an old WPA project, McLain Rogers Park, with a nifty Art Deco entrance.

Clinton Drive-In

Opened: Aug. 17, 1949

Closed: May 3, 1983

Capacity: 256 cars

Location: On Route 66 about two miles south of town, just south of Neptune Park.

The Clinton Drive-In's life almost precisely matched that of its owner, Video Independent Theaters. Technically, it spent its first few months as a Griffith drive-in. The Griffith chain, which at its peak owned dozens of indoor theaters in Oklahoma and northern Texas, was formed by L. C. Griffith with Harry Lowenstein. The latter passed away the day after the Clinton opened, and ill health forced the former to retire the following month. In December 1949, Video Independent Theaters was incorporated from the remains of the Griffith chain. The new organization included the old Griffith theaters and most of the old Griffith employees.

Undated photo from the William B. Turk Collection of the Oklahoma Historical Society via the Gateway to Oklahoma History, https://gateway.okhistory.org.

There were a couple of notable events for the Clinton. It offered an annual fireworks display each Independence Day, but in 1951, a spark from one of the first rockets set off the rest of the cache. The *Clinton Daily News* wrote, "No one was hurt in the premature firing of the display. Those some distance away said it made a very pretty show. Those closer up weren't sure. They were too busy dodging to look." In January 1967, a tornado knocked over the screen, but Video had plenty of time to rebuild it before the season started.

In April 1983, Georgia-based Martin Theatres announced a deal to buy out Video, effective in a few weeks. When the official changeover hit, on May 3 that year, Martin picked through Video's drive-ins to see which ones it wanted to close. The Clinton never reopened, ending its existence on the same day as its owner. A housing development occupies the site today.

Elk City

The National Route 66 Museum is on the west side of Elk City, barely a stone's throw from the old 66 Drive-In site. The museum has an interactive drive-in theater exhibit for those poor souls who have no idea what it's like to watch a movie in a real one. The 20-foot "world's largest Route 66 sign" is out front, so you can't miss it.

66 Drive-In

Opened: April 5, 1949

Closed: 1985?

Capacity: 400 cars

Location: On Route 66 on the west side of town, just a few blocks west of the present-day National Route 66 and Transportation Museum.

The 1960 season opening ad in the *Elk City Daily News* showed off its screen - it may have just been widened.

Griffith Theatres began building the 66 Drive-In in the winter of 1948, hoping to open the following March. They only missed by one month. Griffith manager Dale Brister ran the drive-in its first year. The 66 lived the typically quiet life that came with corporate ownership, as Griffith gave way to Video Independent, which was purchased in 1983 by Martin Theaters, which sort of renamed itself Carmike.

When did the 66 close? An aerial photo from February 1984 showed it intact. Carmike included it in its entry in the 1986 edition of the *Motion Picture Almanac* circuit list, but omitted it in 1987. Since those books were published early each year, I'd guess that the 66 made it through the 1985 season before closing. What was once advertised as "western Oklahoma's largest babysitter" was soon replaced by a Wal-Mart, now a Tractor Supply Company store.

Erick

Despite its small size (fewer than 2000 residents), Erick spawned two famous recording artists. Sheb Wooley reached the top of the charts in 1958 with "The Purple People Eater." The more prolific musician was Roger Miller, whose many hits are topped by "King of the Road."

Bearcat Drive-In

Opened: June 16, 1952

Closed: June 15, 1964

Capacity: 108 cars

Location: On state highway 30 about a mile and a half north of Route 66.

Lamar Guthrie, who owned the Rogue Theatre in Erick, built a very small drive-in north of town. Although it was modern enough to include individual speakers for each car, the Bearcat, named for the local high school mascot, held barely 100 cars. It was the smallest known drive-in on Route 66 and one of the smallest drive-ins ever built anywhere.

With a drive-in that small, it stands to reason that the owner would need a side job or two. For Guthrie, that was the indoor theater, then building and operating cable TV companies in nearby towns. He seemed to fall in love with one of those towns, Hollis, about 35 miles south of Erick, so much that he moved there in 1958. His sister, Lillie Edmondson, ran the Bearcat in Guthrie's absence. He soon advertised his Erick theaters for sale.

A year later, Guthrie was still trying to sell the Bearcat. "Will sell at a figure where it will pay for itself in two years," he wrote. "Will sell on time payment." On Oct. 1, 1959, a local tractor repairman, Garland Dobson, took Guthrie up on that offer. Dobson continued his repair work on the side while Guthrie prospered in Hollis.

By 1962, Amos Page, owner of the Derby Drive-In across the border in McLean TX, booked the movies for the Bearcat, though Mr. and Mrs. Dobson still ran the place. For some reason, their weekly newspaper ads for the drive-in abruptly ceased

New 'Bearcat' Drive-in Theatre

1½ Miles North Erick

OPENING

MONDAY, JUNE 16th

With

OKLAHOMA PREMIERE

MONDAY – TUESDAY SHOWING OF

Randolph Scott in

"Carson City" in color

This is the first showing of this picture in Oklahoma.

Our Policy will be to show **Only New Pictures**, no second runs!

We will bring you the finest there is in pictures – three changes weekly – Monday – Tuesday; Wednesday – Thursday; Friday – Saturday.

The Bearcat's grand opening ad as it appeared in the *Beckham County Democrat*.

in June 1964; the final show mentioned was for Monday, June 15. In November that year, Guthrie announced that he was dismantling the Bearcat, which he had sold to a nearby farmer. "For the last few years, Garland Dobson and his wife have been operating the drive-in," *Boxoffice* reported, "but they closed it a few months ago and Guthrie was unsuccessful in getting another operator to take it over." An oilfield service company sits today at the site of the Bearcat's modest screen.

Intermission:

Concession Stand Evolution

Concession stands at the drive-ins went through a lot of changes, away from old-time theater owners' habits to more profitable alternatives. Some of those habits were informed by the earliest days of indoor theaters.

Walk-up concession stands were once common at drive-ins. The Star Drive-In, built in 1950 in Montrose CO, still keeps theirs that way. Photo © Joe Sohm | Dreamstime.com.

Most of the first indoor movie theaters sold no snacks. Street vendors popped corn in carts in front of theater entrances; the smell of fresh popcorn was as strong a draw then as it is now a century later. Eventually a few of the smarter theater owners brought the vendors inside, leasing their lobby for a cut of the profits. Before long, the even smarter owners set up their own concession stands.

(Remember also that it was very difficult to make popcorn at home until the late 1950s. Then the introduction of the stovetop Jiffy Pop and the lesser-known E-Z Pop gave families the only easy way to make fresh popcorn. Before microwave ovens and Jiffy Pop, the opportunity for a popcorn treat provided a special incentive to go to the movies. But I digress.)

When drive-ins started in the 1930s, some of them omitted concession stands completely. Other early drive-ins contracted with vendors to run the food side of the business. The practice evolved after World War II, when thousands of new drive-ins learned through trial and error which approaches were the most profitable.

First were the stands themselves. The earliest concession stands faced the elements. Customers would walk up, place an order, then a worker would gather the requested items and process the payment. More modern drive-ins enclosed the concession stand, usually with air conditioning. Customers could relax inside a climate-controlled atmosphere, encouraging them to linger and buy more.

Next were the movie programs themselves. Many drive-ins started by showing the same movie, plus shorts and a cartoon, twice a night. Operators soon recognized that double features were smarter, since they provided a natural break for selling to a captive audience.

Armour hot dogs was one of many companies that would provide drive-ins with free concession stand promotional trailers to show during intermission. Soft drink makers such as Coke and Pepsi were more common sponsors in the 1960s and 70s. Photo from the Jan. 10, 1953 *Motion Picture Herald*.

The serving style changed. As much as half of a drive-in's concession volume occurred during intermission, typically 10 minutes. Early experiments with cafeteria-style service spread like wildfire, becoming the norm in just a few years. At the larger drive-ins, patrons would push a tray along a line, adding pre-packaged snacks and drinks as desired, and then pay the cashier at the end.

Another area of change was the menu. Drive-ins originally offered the same snacks as indoor theaters. They soon learned that many of the families who came to the drive-in wanted more than a snack, they wanted a meal. Hamburgers and hot dogs became some of the best sellers. In the 1950s, some drive-ins began offering then-exotic treats such as egg rolls and pizza, sometimes as the only place in town to get that type of food.

On the other hand, drive-in operators discovered that, beyond a certain point, adding food options to the

Modern drive-ins switched to efficient cafeteria-style service, with trays on a long slider past prepackaged snacks and sandwiches on the way to the cashier at the end. 2013 photo by the author of the 88 Drive-In, Commerce City CO.

menu resulted in lower profits. Patrons would pause to consider which option to choose, and in the cafeteria format, the line moves only as quickly as its slowest customer.

Priming the drive-in customer to buy was another important job for savvy drive-in owners. Free playgrounds for children were a way to get them and their parents to arrive early and spend more time at the snack bar. And the concession stand trailers shown during intermission preached to the captive audience that the tastiest food in town was waiting to be purchased.

Concession stand profits kept many drive-ins going, especially when they sold snacks during daylight swap meets. Today they're an important part of a theater's overall bottom line. Next time you visit a drive-in, be sure to buy a bag of popcorn to help keep them alive.

Texas

Thanks to its size and warm climate, Texas had the most drive-ins of any US state. At the industry's peak in the mid-1950s, well over 450 drive-ins called Texas home, more than any other two states combined. At least one of every 10 US drive-ins was in the Lone Star State. You get the idea. But the Mother Road crossed Texas at its panhandle, so there were only eight anywhere close by.

Shamrock

The crown jewel of Shamrock for Route 66 fans, and maybe just in general, is the Conoco Tower Station and U-Drop Inn Café at the northeast corner of 66 and US 83. This gorgeous art deco structure, built in 1936, is listed in the National Register of Historic Places. It's been fully restored; although it no longer sells gas or hash browns, today it hosts Shamrock's Visitor Information Center.

Pioneer Drive-In

Opened: June 14, 1950

Closed: 1975?

Capacity: 300 cars

Location: On Route 66 about a mile east of town.

J. Seibert Worley was a big deal in Shamrock. He ran the indoor Liberty and Texas theaters there, and he would later serve seven terms as mayor. In early 1950, he consulted with drive-in architects in Dallas and Oklahoma City before building his own. The Pioneer, a name chosen in a contest, had a 47½-foot-wide screen on a tower that was 56 feet high. Its concession stand included a patio with tables and chairs, and Worley soon added a playground.

The Pioneer was the kind of standard 300-car drive-in that was common in small towns in the 1950s. Detail of a 1962 USGS photo.

Worley widened the Pioneer's screen in 1956 and remodeled the drive-in in 1966, when his son Jack was managing his theaters and cable TV company. In 1969, Worley added a white attraction board, improved the playground, swapped in new speakers, and repainted the area green and white. In 1974, Worley leased the Pioneer, with an option to buy, for two years to Athel Boyter and Dan Wolfenbarger. Those may have been the drive-in's final seasons. When the *Motion Picture Almanac* refreshed its drive-in list for its 1977 edition, it no longer included the Pioneer. A paved, empty lot occupies the site today.

McLean

Route 66 fans should seek out the Devil's Rope Museum, a celebration of barbed wire. The Texas Route 66 Museum is also part of the same building, which used to house the Form-o-uth Brassiere Company. The prolific output of that company caused McLean city leaders to erect a billboard proclaiming the town "The Uplift Capital of the World".

Derby Drive-In

Opened: Sept. 11, 1952

Closed: July 19, 1973?

Capacity: 130 cars

Location: On Route 66 about a mile east of town.

The front page of the March 6, 1952, *McLean News* promoted a bold idea from Howard Horne, manager of the Southwestern Public Service Company. Horne told the local Jaycees that McLean needed an identifying feature – he never used the word "gimmick." If almost everyone in McLean wore derby hats – "not just for a short-timie fad, but from now on" – then the place would become known as the "Derby City," so tourists driving through on 66 would stop to ask about it and spend

The tiny Derby had a "modern concession stand" according to its *McLean News* grand opening ad.

money. The newspaper would run reminders of this promotion several times in 1952, but by the end of the decade, the "Uplift Capital" motto had won out.

Amos Page and his mother, Madge Page, owned the indoor Avalon Theatre in McLean, and in May 1952, they announced they had selected a drive-in theater site southwest of town. A few months later, they switched to a spot on US 66 just east of the city limits.

Compared to the width of the highway, the Derby's viewing field looked very small in this 1962 photo. © HistoricAerials.com, used by permission.

The Pages had also owned the indoor Lone Star Theatre, which had burned down around 1950. For the drive-in project, they collected bricks from the years-old rubble, hired local boys to clean the bricks, and then reused them to build the concession stand.

The Pages didn't name the drive-in until late August, which suggests how long that local derby fad lasted. The Derby Drive-In opened with just five ramps to hold about 130 cars, but there were in-car speakers for all of them. The brick concession stand also contained the projection booth and rest rooms.

Amos Page mostly left the operation of the Derby to his mother, and that trend accelerated in 1962 when he moved to Quanah TX with his family to run another drive-in near there. By 1967, Madge Page ran the Derby, staying open just three or four months a year, and in 1970, she leased it to Bob Phillips. After the 1972 season, Phillips' main job transferred him to Velma OK, so Page leased the Derby to Mike Williams, a new teacher in

McLean with no theater experience. *Boxoffice* wrote in June 1973 that Williams had some "intriguing ideas" for the drive-in, but the Derby's final ad in the *News* appeared on July 19. Small houses occupy the site today.

Amarillo

Easily the largest city on Route 66 between Oklahoma City and Albuquerque, Amarillo has the only active drive-in near the Mother Road between Tulsa and California. My favorite stop in town is the Big Texas Steak Ranch & Brewery, a wonderfully kitschy western restaurant that will give you a very full dinner with a 72-ounce steak, all for free if you can down every bit within 60 minutes.

Trail Drive-In

Opened: April 29, 1948

Closed: 1982?

Capacity: 400 cars

Location: On Route 66 about two miles east of town.

Wendell Oren "W. O." Bearden switched careers in his late 20s from public school teacher to theater owner. He started in 1936 by opening the indoor Tech Theater in Lubbock, partnered with future Texas governor Preston Smith. In 1947, he began building Amarillo's first drive-in theater on "the English Field Highway" east of town. The initial plans called for an 11-acre site that could hold almost 1000 cars, all facing a 50x50-foot screen tower.

When construction wrapped up the following spring, the field was smaller and the screen was 41x30 feet, but there were several hundred seats near the front and a playground in front of the concession-projection

In 1977, when John Margolies took this photo, the Trail's covered wagon mural was long gone, its paint was fading in spots, but the box office was open for business. From the John Margolies Roadside America photograph archive (1972-2008), Library of Congress, Prints and Photographs Division.

building. The screen tower featured Tex Merrick's huge mural of a covered wagon going down a canyon trail. Bearden installed 400 in-car speakers and said that he could add more if he enlarged the viewing field. The Trail was set to open on April 23, but heavy rain showers washed the gravel off the ramps the day before.

Bearden, who lived in Lubbock until he passed

This grainy 1948 photo from the *Amarillo Globe* showed the Trail's original mural (by Tex Merrick, in progress) and its street sign.

Five years later, Margolies returned to take another picture of the Trail. The box office had new paneling up front; everything else just looked a little more weathered. From the John Margolies Roadside America photograph archive (1972-2008), Library of Congress, Prints and Photographs Division.

away in 1999, apparently owned or co-owned the Trail for the rest of its life. Within a few years after opening, the Trail replaced its elaborate mural with the word "Trail", which must have been easier to maintain. The tower was heavily damaged by fire in June 1966; that might have prompted the switch from the mural.

By 1970, the Trail was showing X-rated films and had stopped advertising in the *Amarillo Globe-Times*. The paper ran a note in 1977 mentioning that the Trail was still showing adult films, and that it had installed a lighting system to prevent passers-by from viewing the screen. And that's all I know for sure about when the Trail closed. John Margolies's 1982 photo of the Trail's screen tower showed the paint deteriorating, but a small admission price sign in the window of the box office. One

Facebook user posted recently that the Trail closed in 1983. The screen tower was gone in a 1991 aerial photo. The site, which still has hints of the drive-in's ramps, sat vacant for decades until a few years ago when a small car dealership moved in.

Skyway Drive-In

Opened: Oct. 27, 1950

Closed: Feb. 22, 1964

Capacity: 550 cars

Location: On US 287, now also I-40, two miles due south of Route 66 and Evergreen Street.

Lester Dollison owned the indoor Rex and Star theaters in Amarillo, as well as others in Sherman, Denton, Wichita Falls, and San Angelo. He moved his company's headquarters to Amarillo in May 1950, and seeing the success of the first three drive-ins there, began building an "ultra modern" version in July. After weeks of delays, the Skyway barely opened in time for the 1950 season. A parachuter, jumping from a plane piloted by the Skyway's manager's brother, delivered the first film for the grand opening.

Within a few years, the group of Charles Weisenberg, John Fagan, and Harold Wilson, who

The Skyway's grand opening ad in the Oct. 27, 1950 *Amarillo Globe*.

together owned the Twin, purchased the Skyway from Dollison. The drive-in had a fairly quiet life until its final few years. The Texas Highway Department wanted to build I-40 over the Skyway's land, but the owners haggled over price. Rather than close the drive-in, they kept it open for just a few weeks each summer to make the land more valuable. By 1962, *Boxoffice* reported that the site was full of snakes and other wildlife. After operating through the winter of 1963, the Skyway's final newspaper ad was on Feb. 21, 1954. Today, the interstate passes over the site of the drive-in's screen; the rest is empty space next to a truck sales lot.

Tascosa Drive-In

Opened: May 2, 1952

~~**Closed:**~~ ~~1987~~ active

Capacity: 800 cars

Location: On US 87 less than a mile north of US 66.

John Margolies' 1977 photo of the Tascosa's original screen. John Margolies Roadside America photograph archive (1972-2008), Library of Congress, Prints and Photographs Division.

The Tascosa is probably the most resilient drive-in that has ever existed on the Mother Road. It has overcome the most difficulties of any ozoner that I know about.

It started as W. O. Bearden's third Amarillo drive-in project, three years after he built the Trail and the Sunset. The Tascosa's first problem was that Bearden and his partner, Leroy Doyle, needed more copper for 800 in-car speaker connections than was allowed by the National Production Authority. They built it anyway. The NPA's penalty, imposed months after the Tascosa opened, was to block Bearden and Doyle from building any other drive-ins for about a year. The partnership's small circuit of theaters would soon be known as the Crossroads Company.

The Tascosa's original viewing field, facing its original, stately screen tower, was on the north side. In 1967, its owners carved off a couple of rows in the back and built a southern viewing field facing a new screen, the one that survives today. Photo © HistoricAerials.com, used by permission.

Doyle settled in to run Crossroads' Amarillo theaters including the Tascosa, which lived the next decade quietly. Its stately screen tower included an indoor screening room, and Crossroads soon enlarged the screen for wider movies. A report in the winter of 1956 noted that the drive-in had a special ring for cowboys and their horses, complete with heaters ready to mount on their saddle horns. The expansion of US 87 into a divided highway in 1962 sliced a piece off the Tascosa's viewing field and turned a previously easy entrance into a maze of detours for the better part of two seasons.

The Tascosa's entryway and attractions board were still showing the effects of the damage from a March 2019 windstorm a couple of months later when this photo was taken by the author.

Crossroads opened a second, south screen in the summer of 1967. The drive-in was advertised as the Tascosa Twin for a decade until a 1978 fire destroyed the original screen tower. That larger screen was never rebuilt, and the Tascosa limped along with only its newer screen until the drive-in closed in 1987.

What was left of the Tascosa's main viewing field was sold off for an RV park, and the south section lay dormant. Then in 1999, Rhett Butler Burns got the idea to reopen the Tascosa. The RV park included the original projection/concession building, so Burns and his family had to build a new one from scratch along with clearing and regraveling the south lot. The drive-in reopened on June 25, 1999.

The next Tascosa disaster hit in July 2004, when a mid-afternoon thunderstorm toppled the screen, smashing the merry-go-round in the playground. Burns rebuilt it all in about a month. Then in March 2019, another windstorm tore off pieces of its entrance towers and the marquee between them. Burns and company fixed those cosmetic problems, then listed the Tascosa for sale in August 2020. The drive-in remained open, and at press time, its web site stated it will reopen for the 2022 season.

Twin Drive-In

Opened: July 18, 1952

Closed: 1989?

Capacity: 1000 cars

Location: On US 60 at Austin Street about 2.9 miles south of Business Route 66 (6th Avenue).

Charles Weisenburg, John Fagan, and Harold Wilson had built Amarillo's second drive-in, the Palo Duro. It must have been extremely successful, because they built its competitor, an even larger drive-in, just across the highway. The Twin had two screens, as you might expect. One tower, backed against the future Canyon Expressway (US 60-87), had 15-foot letters outlined in neon.

Weisenburg wrote a full-page article in the May 2, 1953 issue of *Boxoffice* explaining how his high hopes for economic benefits from twin-screen drive-ins had been dashed. Two screens cost twice as much as a single screen, of course. The expected cost savings of shared concession-projection buildings were more than canceled out by the necessity of second-story projection rooms with stronger equipment for the longer "throws" from the back rows to the screens. Extra signage was needed to direct patrons to their desired movie. "If I were building a drive-in theatre at the moment," he concluded, "it would not be a twin."

The Twin also had its share of weather problems. Gusty winds tore off a large chunk of one screen in April 1958, but the drive-in stayed open. Then in May 1972, a malfunction in the main screen's neon sparked a blaze that destroyed the tower and its storeroom. Fagan, still the manager after 20 years, replaced it with a metal tower a month later.

Fagan passed away in January 1973, and longtime Weisenburg employee Paul McDonald took over the Twin. He announced in

The Twin's grand opening ad in the July 18, 1952, *Amarillo Daily News*.

June 1975 that he would replace the old south wooden screen tower, damaged by wind and rain, with a metal tower that matched the main screen. He stayed on through at least 1978, when Weisenburg retired and sold all his theaters except the Twin, which he was still leasing to McDonald.

The Twin's history in the 1980s is a little murky. Joseph Dydzak, part of Dydzak Drive-In Theatres Ltd. of Hamilton, Ontario, bought the Twin from Cinemark early in the decade. Dydzak passed away in May 1983, and Wal-Mart subsequently bought the land, but when did the Twin close? Aerial photos show that the screens were gone by 1991, and the site was still a vacant lot of empty ramps as late as 2004. A Wal-Mart Supercenter, built by 2008, is still there today.

Palo-Duro Drive-In

Opened: May 13, 1948

Closed: Nov. 26, 1967

Capacity: 533 cars and 100 seats

Location: On US 60 at Georgia Street about 2.9 miles south of Business Route 66 (6th Avenue).

Charles Weisenburg bought a small indoor theater in Tulia TX when he was just 21. After serving in World War II, Weisenburg happened to visit an east Texas drive-in's grand opening, and he was impressed by the overflow crowds. In 1948, he sold the indoor theater to his brother and teamed with a couple of former film salesmen, John Fagan and Harold Wilson, to form WFW Theatres. Their first big project was the Palo-Duro, which missed being the first drive-in in Amarillo by just a couple of weeks.

The Palo-Duro's screen tower started plain, with just the all-caps words "PALO-DURO" and "THEATRE," with "DRIVE-IN' in smaller letters in the middle. In the lot, each speaker pole had a small, shaded light to help with parking. In 1952, WFW expanded the lot, increasing its capacity from 400 to 533 cars. The next year, WFW enlarged the screen for wider movies. That might have been when it also added a full mural to the

The Palo-Duro Drive-In, left, was so successful that four years later, its owners built the Twin across the highway from it. Photo © HistoricAerials.com, used by permission.

screen tower, keeping the same lettering, with the smaller "DRIVE-IN," running across the top.

In 1954, Fagan and Wilson sold their shares of the drive-in to Weisenberg, but Fagan continued to manage it. Except for occasional vandalism, the Palo-Duro lived the rest of its life fairly quietly. Its 20-year lease ran out in 1967, and the Palo-Duro was razed just a week after it shut down. Today a Randall County office building and the Texas Panhandle War Memorial occupy the site.

Sunset Drive-In

Opened: June 3, 1949

Closed: Nov. 7, 1976

Capacity: 400 cars

Location: On Business Route 66 a couple of blocks east of Veterans Hospital on the west side of town.

The Sunset had been closed only a few months when John Margolies took this 1977 photo. From the John Margolies Roadside America photograph archive (1972-2008), Library of Congress, Prints and Photographs Division.

John Blocker, who once owned the indoor Texas Theater in Abilene, must have loved building drive-ins. In the summer of 1948, he built the Yucca Drive-In in Clovis NM, then sold it in less than two months. Later that year, he went to Wichita Falls TX and built the Falls Drive-In, which he sold after two years. In 1949, Blocker turned to Amarillo, where he built and opened the Sunset, the city's third drive-in. By mid-July, he sold the Sunset to W. O. Bearden, who also owned the Trail on the opposite side of town.

By 1970, the Sunset was showing X-rated movies, and nearby residents asked the city commissioners to ban them from unshielded outdoor screens. The city tabled a proposed ordinance to that effect when the Sunset and other drive-ins agreed to stop showing them. In 1974, a sufficiently provocative R-rated movie prompted the Sunset neighbors to return to the commission, but the drive-in again promised that it would only show G and PG movies from then on. Which wasn't very long; the Sunset closed after the 1976 season. An apartment complex occupies the site today.

Intermission:
The Trail That Wasn't

This is the story of the photo of a Route 66 drive-in that really wasn't a photo of a Route 66 drive-in, and how I found out what it really was. (Yes, I am bragging, just a little.)

Let's start with John Margolies, an architectural critic, author, and most importantly, photographer. Margolies took thousands of photos of roadside architecture in the late 20th century. In 2016, the Library of Congress, which had acquired many of his slides,

Texas

The photo originally marked as Amarillo's Trail. Compare it to the Trail photos 10 pages ago. From the John Margolies Roadside America photograph archive (1972-2008), Library of Congress, Prints and Photographs Division.

created the John Margolies Roadside America Photograph Archive, which is essentially in the public domain.

Margolies captured the images of many signs and screen towers, and I'm happy to say that some of them are in this book. But one picture from the collection bugged me. It's the picture at the top of this Intermission, the Trail. Its description said this was a picture of the Trail Drive-In in Amarillo.

There's no way that photo was of Amarillo's Trail. Look at the movies listed — *Sharky's Machine* was released in December 1981, matching the picture's notes saying it was taken in 1982. Margolies also took a 1982 photo of the real Trail tower, which looks nothing like the thin metal screen above. Considering that Amarillo's Trail was reduced to showing X-rated movies in the 1980s, it's unbelievable that the drive-in's owner would spend the money to build a new screen and show general-release movies in 1982.

What was left of the Athens Trail Drive-In in 2011. Photo by Marty Yawnick / Lifeinlofi.com, used by permission.

Since that picture wasn't taken in Amarillo, where was it taken? That question led me to Cinema-Treasures.org, where a search showed 30 exact matches for "Trail Drive-In," including 14 in Texas. I was checking each drive-in's closing date when I got lucky. A CT user had uploaded a 2011 photo of the remaining frame of the Athens TX Trail's former screen, and the five letter rectangles were a perfect match. The Athens Trail stayed open until 1985, which also lined up. As a bonus, it's easy to imagine a smudged "Athens TX" note being mistaken for Amarillo TX.

I submitted all of this work to the Library of Congress in early 2019. A few weeks later the LoC corrected its record for that picture and credited me for the find.

If someone (perhaps you, dear reader) can find that double feature advertised in a 1982 edition of the *Athens Daily Review*, then we'll know for sure. For now, I'm pretty certain that the metal-screen Trail photo doesn't belong in a Route 66 book. Except in an Intermission like this.

New Mexico

There are stretches of Route 66 where I look at some of the decent-sized towns and wonder why no one ever built a drive-in there. In New Mexico, it's more common for me to wonder how its limited population could support so many drive-ins.

Tucumcari

The city promoted itself with "Tucumcari tonight" billboards along the Mother Road, promising decent rooms in otherwise sparsely populated eastern New Mexico. Among the most impressive of the survivors from that time are the Blue Swallow Motel, a gorgeous facility built in 1939, and the Motel Safari, filled with Route 66 memorabilia.

County / No Name Drive-In

Opened: Oct. 29, 1948

Closed: 1957?

Capacity: 400 cars

Location: Just south of Route 66 on the western edge of town, where Mesalands Community College is now.

John Hasten Snow, who owned and operated the two indoor theaters in Hinton OK, decided in 1948 to build his first drive-in in Tucumcari, over 300 miles west. He started relatively late in the year, which explains why the County Drive-In didn't open until almost the end of October. From the start, it boasted 400 individual speakers and a wide concession-projection building.

Snow reopened the County for the 1949 season, but Loren Yessler owned the place by the start of the 1950 season. My other notes about Loren showed him working in garages in Amarillo, but his wife, Bertha Yessler, was postmaster of Nara Visa NM. Bertha was later appointed justice of the peace there – the first woman to hold that position in state history.

Back to the County. Local man Waldo V. Slusher bought the drive-in, but probably not its land, around 1952. A few years later, Slusher moved to California. Arthur Salcido bought the County from him before the 1954 season. However, Salcido's County ran into financial difficulties in 1955 and appears to have closed in mid-season.

The No Name Drive-In, "formerly the County Drive-In / under new management," began advertising in the *Tucumcari News* in August 1956. Those ads continued into 1957, so that may be when the

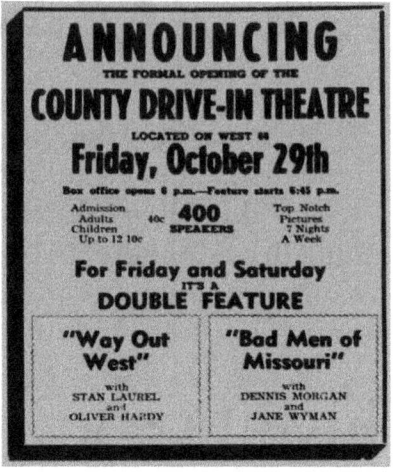

The County's grand opening ad in the *Tucumcari Daily News*.

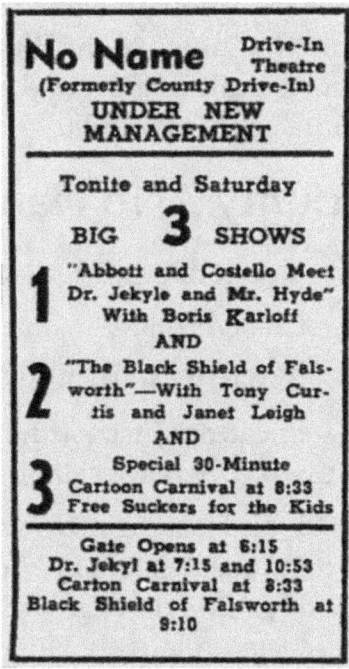

Early No Name ads noted that this had been the County Drive-In.

drive-in closed for good. In March 1960, Tucumcari's school board voted to buy 32 acres of "the Yessler property" for a new high school, which began construction weeks later on the east side of the land. In 1979, New Mexico authorized a vocational school in Tucumcari, and they built the future Mesalands Community College where the County's viewing field had been.

Canal Drive-In

Opened: April 20, 1951

Closed: July 4, 1972

Capacity: 550 cars and 250 seats

Location: On Route 66 about two miles west of town.

Longtime Tucumcari exhibitor Milas Hurley couldn't have been pleased when an out-of-town entrepreneur built the County Drive-In. Hurley didn't rush to respond, eventually choosing a drive-in site farther west of town and starting construction in September 1950. The Canal, named for the Conchas Canal that formed the site's southern border, was scheduled to open on Easter, March 25, but its grand opening ad didn't appear in the *Tucumcari News* until almost a month later.

Motion Picture Herald reported that this was the sign model Milas Hurley bought for the Canal from Poblocki & Sons.

The Canal held 550 cars, and its concession stand included a small auditorium to seat about 200 patrons "in case of stormy or cold weather." The manager lived in an on-site apartment with a switch to light up the viewing field if he heard shenanigans in the night. The whole site was surrounded by a stone wall, giving it an unusual appearance of permanence.

The Canal was named for the Conchas Canal, clearly visible in this 1967 photo. © HistoricAerials.com, used by permission.

Poblocki and Sons of Milwaukee trucked down and installed its 30-foot-high sign.

Hurley, who was once president of the New Mexico Theatres Association, seemed to know what he was doing. The County flipped through ownership changes and reboots while the Canal prospered. In 1963, Hurley sold all of his Tucumcari theaters to Frontier Theatres. Six years later, Commonwealth Theatres bought the Frontier chain, and Commonwealth owned the Canal for the rest of its life, which wasn't all that long. Commonwealth dropped the Canal from its *News* ads in the first week of July 1972.

Although a truck stop initially replaced the Canal, the site sits vacant today, without a trace of the drive-in that spent two decades there.

Santa Rosa

Thanks to the Blue Hole, an 81-foot deep natural well, Santa Rosa is known as "The Scuba Diving Capital of the Southwest." The town's "Fat Man" cartoon portrait, originally for the Club Café and rescued in 1991 by Joseph's Bar and Grill, has been a Route 66 landmark since 1935.

Sky-Ranch Drive-In

Opened: Aug. 15, 1952

Closed: 1962?

Capacity: 200 cars

Location: On US 54 less than half a mile south of Route 66 on the west side of town.

In the 1930s, Lester Dollison put together a little circuit of indoor theaters, mostly in Texas. By 1944, he was running the Studio in Vaughn NM, about 40 miles from Santa Rosa, and he enjoyed the cooler evenings there. In 1948, Dollison bought the Pecos in Santa Rosa. He also opened a couple of drive-ins elsewhere, including the Skyway in Amarillo, before turning to southwest Santa Rosa.

On the day the Sky-Ranch opened, the pages of the *Santa Rosa News* were dominated by a different new facility, Guadalupe General Hospital. In the back was the grand opening notice for the drive-in,

The Sky-Ranch's grand opening ad in the *Santa Rosa News*.

boasting a "mammoth screen." The *Theatre Catalog* listed the "Sky Ranch" (no hyphen) with a capacity of 200 cars; *Motion Picture Almanac* had it with 250.

The Sky-Ranch looked intact in a 1962 aerial photo, but a May 1962 issue of the *News* included only the Pecos, nothing for a drive-in. Dollison stayed in Santa Rosa for a while, renaming the Pecos as the Rodeo in 1965, but there were never any other mentions of the Sky-Ranch. Although it was still intact in a 1973 photo, the screen was gone by 1983. Today scattered housing occupies the site, just north of the new Guadalupe County Hospital.

Albuquerque

Although there are a plethora of Route 66 landmarks in Albuquerque, I have a few historic favorites. The Kimo Theatre, built in 1925, stands less than a block from the intersection of the original 66 path down 4th Street and the more recent version along Central Avenue. Old Town's central plaza, established three centuries ago, is just a block away from the Mother Road. And the Dog House in between still makes my favorite chili dogs.

Other Albuquerque drive-ins more than three miles from Route 66: Albuquerque 6 (1978-1995), Silver Dollar Twin (1963-1980), Star / Linda Vista / Northside (1949-1988). Also not included: Circle Autoscope (1963-1963?).

Terrace Drive-In

Opened: Oct. 18, 1951

Closed: Jan. 20, 1980

Capacity: 1600 cars

Location: On Route 66 (Central Avenue) on the east side of town.

Tom Griffing was a prolific drive-in builder for other owners, and occasionally he would keep one for himself. So it was with the Terrace, named for the terrace of 400 lounge chairs that Griffing provided for patrons who wanted to leave their cars. Despite Korean War-time restrictions on the use of certain materials, Griffing kept the project under the copper maximum (barely) by running heavy wiring directly from the poles to the top of the projection booth, on top of the concession stand at the back of the viewing field. There wasn't enough copper left to reach the exit lights, so the Terrace got by with kerosene lanterns until they were free to run more wiring.

The Terrace was named for the outdoor terrace seating available for walk-ins and patrons who didn't want to watch the movies from their cars. Photo from the *Motion Picture Herald*.

Just a year later, Griffing added a second screen, advertising the drive-in as the Terrace Twin. For the first few decades, the Terrace would show the same double feature on both screens, playing one movie first on one screen, the other movie first on the second screen. The expansion doubled the drive-in's capacity to 1600 cars, large enough to stage several "drive-in world premieres" over the years.

In early 1963, Griffing's All-States Theatres sold its 11 drive-ins in New Mexico and Texas to Oklahoma-based Video Independent Theatres. The new owners rewired the car speakers in 1968 and fixed tornado damage on its neon sign in 1969. Finally, in 1975, Video recognized that it could run completely separate double

The highlight of the Terrace was its neon-outlined dancing woman, 70 feet high and 50 feet wide, on the screen tower. Just a hint of that color remained in this 1979 photo © Steve Fitch, used by permission.

features on its two screens. The Terrace closed for the season in January 1980, and didn't reopen. A mobile home park occupies the site today.

    I saved the best part of the Terrace for last. Artist Keith Kent designed and neon worker Doug Mason constructed "a queen of the tubes, an empress of electricity, who presided over this phosphorescent firmament" as the *Albuquerque Journal* later remembered it. A 70-foot-high dancing woman dazzled decades of patrons, and I'd love to see more color photos of that.

Wyoming Drive-In

Opened: Jan. 26, 1962

Closed: Sept. 18, 1978

Capacity: 1000 cars

Location: On Route 66 (Central Avenue), adjacent to the Terrace.

As Albuquerque grew in the 1950s, the Terrace Drive-In eventually became an unincorporated enclave, surrounded by the city. That's probably why the Wyoming was built as a separate drive-in instead of the Terrace's third screen – it was always within the city limits. Tom Griffing came out of semi-retirement to build the Wyoming, which had a 120x60-foot screen and a four-lane cafeteria-style concession stand. *Boxoffice* reported in November 1961 that the drive-in had opened on Thanksgiving Day, but the announcement was premature.

Griffing's company, All-States Theatres, owned the Wyoming for barely a year before selling it with their other 10 drive-ins to Oklahoma-based Video Independent Theatres. Just before Christmas 1967, strong winds smashed over 500 feet of the Wyoming's fence and broke some glass.

Though the Wyoming, left, was adjacent to the Terrace Twin Drive-In, it was within the Albuquerque city limits while the Terrace wasn't. 1967 photo © HistoricAerials.com, used by permission

Video resurfaced the lot along with the Terrace's in 1968. In early 1969, parts of the fence were blown down again.

The Wyoming closed at the end of the 1978 season, a victim of rising land values. A mobile home park occupies the site today.

Tesuque Drive-In

Opened: Aug. 7, 1949

Closed: Dec. 13, 1977

Capacity: 656 cars

Location: At the corner of Pennsylvania Avenue and what was then Tesuque Street, about a half mile north of Route 66 (Central Avenue).

The Tesuque, Albuquerque's second drive-in, went through more changes than any other drive-in in New Mexico. When it opened, it had a single screen facing north and a narrow lot that held just 368 cars. Business was so good that in 1952, owners Clifford and Helen

The sturdy-looking, humble, original screen tower for the Tesuque as construction neared completion in 1949. Looks like it had a manager's apartment at its base. Photo courtesy of the Albuquerque Museum.

The shifting configurations of the Tesuque, as told in aerial photos. It started small (1951 photo, left), added a second screen in the northeast corner but removed it (1959, center), then shifted the single screen tower to point northeast (1967, right). Photos © HistoricAerials.com, used by permission.

Butler made a deal with Helen's brother, Earle E. Unger, to finance an expansion that included a second screen. The couple would later say that they agreed to let Unger represent himself as sole owner of the Tesuque to facilitate loans; I'm sure Unger told a different story.

In 1953, the Tesuque expanded to two screens serving 850 cars. That was also the year Unger incorporated the Tesuque Drive-In Theatres, with himself as president, his wife as vice-president, manager W. T. Marshall as secretary-treasurer, and the Butlers left out. The couple sued. In July 1954, a court ruled that the Butlers' real estate contracts with Unger were legitimate, so the Tesuque corporation won. The Butlers divorced in January 1956.

I'm not sure whether it was related to the aftermath of the lawsuit, but 1954 was also when the Tesuque was sold to Sunset Drive-In owner Marlin Butler, apparently no relation to Clifford. In February 1956, a windstorm tore off a section of the Tesuque Twin's east screen. Butler rebuilt the east screen later that year, but scrapped it for the 1957 season.

The removal of the second screen left a viewing area with a lot of cars off at an angle to the remaining screen. The Tesuque fixed this with the unusual step of rotating its screen about 45 degrees to face northeast. In 1958, Butler also enlarged the concession stand to reflect the larger field. At the end of 1963, he sold the Tesuque to Frontier Theatres on a lease-purchase agreement. Commonwealth Theatres bought out Frontier in 1968. By 1971, it was running the Tesuque as a cut-rate dollar theater.

The Tesuque had been built in a vacant area outside of town, but through the decades, housing had expanded to surround the site. By the mid-1970s, the neighborhood association lobbied the city to buy and close the drive-in, called a blight "because of ugly signs and because it attracts persons from outside the neighborhood." Those neighbors got their wish in 1978; the local Urban Development Agency used federal funds to acquire the Tesuque, which it converted to Mesa Verde Park and Community Center, still there today.

Duke City Drive-In

Opened: Feb. 17, 1953

Closed: Sept. 3, 1979

Capacity: 600 cars

Location: On Carlisle Boulevard, about 2.2 miles north of Route 66 (Central Avenue).

In October 1952, on the first anniversary of the opening of the Terrace, owner Tom Griffing announced that he would build another Albuquerque drive-in. Construction proceeded faster than anticipated and only cool weather delayed the opening until mid-February.

The *Albuquerque Progress*, published by the Albuquerque National Bank, ran this photo of the freshly built Duke City.

The Duke City Drive-In, a moniker chosen for a nickname of its host city, included red-lighted stop signs along a center pedestrian path. The concession stand featured modern self-service. The projection booth was future-proofed with facilities for 3D and TV-based projectors, although those fads died out within a few years.

In the summer of 1953, manager George Fossell demonstrated the sprayers on every speaker post for the *Albuquerque Journal*. Workers used the sprayers to distribute a disinfectant-insecticide mixture every day that summer, which took four hours a day to get through all 600 spots in the viewing lot.

The Duke City lived a relatively quiet life, owned by Griffing's All-States Theatres. Oklahoma-based Video Independent Theatres bought All-States' drive-ins in early 1963. Video installed a self-service car wash out front in 1964, planted hundreds of trees in a 1966 landscaping project, added an exit guard in 1968, and repaired the flexiboard on the screen tower after a 1969 storm. The Duke City quietly closed on Labor Day 1979, then didn't reopen in 1980. A Wal-Mart occupies the site today.

Cactus Drive-In

Opened: Sept. 26, 1947

Closed: Sept. 28, 1975

Capacity: 680 cars

Location: On Yale Boulevard, about 1.2 miles south of Route 66 (Central Avenue).

The first drive-in in New Mexico was built by George Tucker and Albuquerque Theaters in late 1947. Its sturdy screen tower was made of welded steel pipes, with a manager's office, storage space, and a three-room caretaker's apartment at the base. On the screen side, a children's playground and outdoor seating faced a 45x55-foot screen. Its concession stand, 250 feet away in the center of the fourth ramp, was decorated in green and coral.

When the Cactus opened, patrons would buy tickets at the box office, then drive around a cactus garden to ushers who would direct them to their parking spaces, equipped with RCA in-car speakers. In 1949, the Cactus added in-car heaters.

The drive-in's following ownership changes confuse me. By 1956, Henry Griffith was president of Albuquerque Exhibitors, which owned the Cactus among others. In January that year, Dallas-based Frontier Theaters, of which Griffith was also president, bought Albuquerque Exhibitors. In 1959, Video Independent Theatres of Oklahoma began operating the Cactus. Then in the summer of 1962, Albuquerque Theatres, still a subsidiary of Frontier, took over the Cactus from All-States Theatres. Commonwealth Theatres bought out Frontier in 1968, and that's who owned the Cactus when it closed.

New Mexico

In 1979, the Cactus screen tower still looked impressive, but signs of decay were noticeable. From the John Margolies Roadside America photograph archive (1972-2008), Library of Congress, Prints and Photographs Division.

The drive-in's gorgeous screen tower stayed up for several years after the Cactus closed. In 1983, the city of Albuquerque bought the site to replace the Heights Community Center. Today the Loma Linda Community Center lives there, with faint hints of the drive-in's back ramps on the east side.

San Jose / Tri-C / Route 25 Drive-In

Opened: Feb. 23, 1954

Closed: June 18, 1965

Capacity: 400 cars

Location: On Broadway, about 2.8 miles south of Route 66.

Robert Morley owned a small piece of Albuquerque's Sunset Drive-In. It must have been doing well because in September 1953, he began building his own drive-in on the east side of the Rio Grande. Morley claimed that the San Jose's screen, 85x70 feet, was one of the largest in the Southwest, and that its lot would hold 600 cars. By the time the drive-in opened, its size was scaled back to 400 cars.

The San Jose started with a policy of double features including one Spanish-language movie and one in English. By the summer of 1955, it occasionally showed what the Catholic Legion of Decency called "very dirty" movies, which Morley defended as "highly educational" hygiene films. In September 1956, the San Jose was hit with an injunction against allegedly indecent films.

In the spring of 1957, Morley sold the San Jose to Carl Halberg, who renamed it the Tri-C. Just a few weeks later, winds blew down chunks of the screen, which Halberg quickly patched. In October 1957, the New Mexico Supreme Court overruled the previous year's injunction because the relevant statute didn't apply to movies.

In the summer of 1961, Halberg leased the Tri-C to Sero Amusement of Los Angeles, which ran it for about two years. In the spring of 1963, winds knocked down the old screen, and Halberg replaced it with a metal screen, reopening in June as the Route 25 Drive-In. The

This *Albuquerque Progress* cover showed the scale of the San Jose's screen. Photo courtesy of the Albuquerque Museum.

site's high winds had the last laugh just two years later, pushing that metal screen backward at a 45-degree angle on the night of June 18, 1965. Apparently that was when Halberg gave up. The Route 25 never ran another ad in the *Albuquerque Journal* after that night, and a 1967 aerial photo showed the site overgrown. A truck salvage yard is there today.

Sunset Drive-In

Opened: Nov. 28, 1951

Closed: Sept. 25, 1988

Capacity: 400 cars

Location: At the corner of Arenal Road and Isleta Boulevard, about 2.5 miles due south of Route 66's bridge over the Rio Grande.

Longtime theater owner Marlin Butler announced at the end of August 1951 that the National Production Authority had granted him permission to build a small drive-in to serve the Armijo neighborhood. The Sunset was built in three months, opening on the Wednesday after Thanksgiving.

The Sunset lived a quiet life for a few years until Butler leased or sold it to Carl and Phyllis Halberg, who purchased the San Jose / Tri-C across the river in 1957. In 1963, Sero Amusement of California, the company booking the Tri-C's movies, ran into local opposition to their racy content. Around the same time, residents near the Sunset, which happened to be just outside the city limits, also complained about that drive-in's similar content. Phyllis told the *Albuquerque Journal* that "an out of town company" was booking the Sunset's movies, and a few weeks later, Carl issued a statement that he had ended that "lease arrangement with an unnamed man in California."

By the end of 1963, Butler's business partner Fred Morley filed a lawsuit against the Halbergs seeking to reclaim the Sunset. That must have worked out, because Commonwealth-Frontier Theatres bought the Sunset from Butler in August 1968. Under Commonwealth, the

The Sunset's sign continues to hang in there, though it looks a little worse for wear every year. It's still there today, though the wooded area and the drive-in's ramps behind it were recently leveled. 2019 photo by the author.

drive-in showed mostly Spanish-language movies, and it closed at the end of the 1981 season.

Someone reopened the Sunset in 1987, showing mostly English-language movies. The 1988 *Motion Picture Almanac* listed the owner as D. Armino, but I haven't found anything else about that person. The Sunset closed again, this time for good, after the 1988 season. The screen and the remains of the marquee are still there today, although its concession stand and ramps were leveled in late 2020.

66 Drive-In

Opened: Aug. 30, 1949

Closed: June 25, 1983

Capacity: 750 cars

Location: On Route 66 (Central Avenue) on the west side of town.

The December 1949 issue of *Albuquerque Progress* published this photo of the recently completed 66. Photo courtesy of the Albuquerque Museum.

Albuquerque Theatres, led by George Armstrong, must have liked the response to the city's first two drive-ins, because they soon jumped on the bandwagon. In February 1949, George Tucker said that the 66 Drive-In, at the entrance to the old West Mesa Airport, would hold about 750 to 1000 cars. In April, he added that the drive-in would open with electric in-car heaters, and in May, he dropped the planned capacity to 550 cars. That was its size when the 66 opened, complete with a patio next to the snack bar for patrons who wanted to watch the movie outside their cars.

In the early years, before more competing drive-ins opened, the 66 often played to capacity crowds. Its ad in the June 11, 1951 *Albuquerque Journal* boasted that the drive-in had added room for another 200 cars as a result. That would probably mark the high point in the 66's history.

In the spring of 1957, just six years after the 66 expanded its viewing field, Albuquerque Theatres replaced it with the "66 Micro-Midget Race Track," a tenth-mile car-racing oval and grandstands costing $150,000. That fad didn't last long. In the summer of 1962, the company announced that, with more folks moving to the west side of town, it would effectively rebuild the 66 as a drive-in again. By the time it reopened in July 1964, Frontier Theatres had bought the place. Frontier installed a new sign and a new 50x100-foot screen.

In 1968, Commonwealth Theatres bought out Frontier, including the 66. Around 1980, Commonwealth subleased the drive-in to Texas National Theaters, which emphasized "skin flicks" in its nightly shows. Prompted by

The rebuilding of the 66 in the 1960s included a new sign outlined in neon. 1969 photo posted by Michigandriveins.com at CinemaTreasures.org.

unhappy neighbors, the city of Albuquerque said the drive-in was operating in violation of the zoning code, which prohibited adult entertainment within 500 feet of residences, churches, or schools. In September 1980, the city obtained a permanent injunction against showing such films, and the state supreme court upheld the injunction in January 1982.

Texas National soon struck back, requesting the city's permission to divide its land, which would put the theater section far enough away from nearby residences. When that failed, the company filed a federal lawsuit asserting it had a First Amendment right to choose what it showed. The city reached a settlement with Texas National that summer, agreeing to assume the remaining two years of the company's lease at a cost of $145,000. Racing returned to the site for those two summers; the park department used it as a BMX dirt bike track.

The 66 sat idle for years after the city's lease expired. In the 1990s, a food distribution company built a warehouse in the back of the field; two expansions later, it's still there today.

Grants

Three brothers, Angus, John, and Lewis Grant, got the contract to build the Atlantic and Pacific Railroad through here in the 1880s. It became a uranium boom town in the 1950s, and the iconic Uranium Café opened there in 1956. The city now has a drive-through neon Route 66 sign that looks especially good after dark.

Sahara Drive-In

Opened: May 1958

Closed: June 1964

Capacity: 300 cars

Location: On Route 66 near Sakelares Boulevard on the east side of town.

Jerome "J.C." West's career in the movie business started in Big Spring TX, where he projected films on a white building wall and pumped sound from two large speakers hung from trees. His Terrace Drive-In there was a big hit. Looking to expand, West came to Grants in 1950 and bought the indoor Lux Theatre. After building the Trails west of town in 1953 (see below), he must have liked how well it performed. West's next move was to build the Sahara on the east side of Grants.

A rare look at the Sahara sign in action, posted by CinemaTreasures.org member Nlister.

Whether from inertia or an effort by the new owners to preserve a bit of history, the remnants of the Sahara sign remain in place today. 2019 photo by the author.

The Sahara was a decent-sized drive-in, with room for 300 or 400 cars, depending on the source, and a 58x90-foot screen. After the Sahara was finished, West built his indoor showcase, named the West Theatre, in 1959. (The West is still active there on old Route 66 today.)

Maybe the small Grants-Milan market could only support one drive-in. For whatever reason, the Sahara operated for barely six years; West shuttered the place in the summer of 1964. After a few years, a trash transfer station moved in and set up shop in the back of the viewing field. All that's left of the drive-in today is the bottom half of the Sahara sign and marquee at its old entrance on 66.

Milan

In 1957, landowner Salvador Milan wanted to be annexed by Grants, but the city was unable to buy the water company that served his property. Instead, the village of Milan formed that year. The Motel Milan, another Route 66 icon, was built in 1946 and restored as a trading post decades later.

Trails Drive-In

Opened: March 1954?

Closed: 1984?

Capacity: 300 cars

Location: Two blocks west of Route 66 at East Street.

J.C. West came to Grants from Big Spring TX in 1950 (see above), and his first construction project was the Trails Drive-In, then about two miles west of town. In April 1953, he told *Boxoffice* magazine that he had bought $15,000 worth of equipment for the drive-in. In early September, *Boxoffice* wrote that the Trails would open later that month, but in January 1954, the magazine said it would open "early in the spring." The 1954 opener could have just been a season opener, but my guess is that delays pushed the opener past the September 1953 target to the following season.

When it was built, the Trails was west of the Grants city limits. It looked remote in this sign photo, posted by CinemaTreasures.org member Nlister.

The Trails was small, about one small city block, though it was in the middle of nowhere when it was built. It had a wide screen facing northeast. Patrons would pay at the single box office at the back of the field, closest to Route 66.

By 1981, housing had surrounded the Trails. © HistoricAerials.com, used by permission.

It sounds like West grew tired of running the Grants-Milan theaters. He opened an indoor theater in Albuquerque, and in 1975, he and a partner opened a recording studio there. West started his next career in music, as a promoter, manager, and sound engineer for bands. In January 1977, Theatre Operators, based in Bozeman MT, leased the Grants-Milan theaters and eventually bought them.

The Trails was still operating in 1983, when the *Albuquerque Journal* mentioned it in passing. In September 1984, Theatre Operators sold the drive-in to former city manager Roy McDowell. I'm not certain that the Trails was still active then, and I don't know whether McDowell ever reopened it. Hints of the old ramps and the concession stand foundation are still there today.

Gallup

Gallup, the biggest city between Albuquerque and Flagstaff on Route 66, is home to the El Rancho Hotel. For decades, Hollywood filmmakers used the El Rancho as their base for dozens of productions such as *Billy the Kid* (1930) and *Ace in the Hole* (1951). Gallup is also the only place in New Mexico mentioned in Bobby Troup's classic song, "(Get Your Kicks on) Route 66."

Zuni Drive-In

Opened: June 4, 1957

Closed: Oct. 3, 1981

Capacity: 578 cars

Location: On Route 66 on the east side of town.

Longtime Gallup theater man William Nagle oversaw the construction of the Zuni for the Frontier Theatres chain. When it opened, the drive-in sign looked a lot like an old-style Holiday Inn sign, but with the curled arrow cutting between the words instead of going across the top. Less than three months later, lightning shorted the sound system, but Frontier repaired the system in one day.

In 1968, Commonwealth Theatres bought out Frontier, including the Zuni. The city's addition of Aztec Avenue between 66 and the drive-in cut through its old entrance driveway, leaving the screen almost adjacent to the new road. In the 1970s, Zuni manager Bob Sanford attracted patrons with promotions such as "Lucky License Night," a watermelon eating contest, and a "Car Smash Night" featuring sledgehammers and a junker automobile.

This grainy photo, which appeared in the June 4, 1957, *Gallup Independent*, is the only image I've found of the Zuni's sign.

The stumps of the Zuni's wooden screen supports and a brush-covered field ending in a ragged, rocky ridge continue to provide a hint of what a night at the movies there must have been like. 2019 photo by the author.

As the years passed, the Zuni sometimes showed racier films. Its final newspaper ad was for a special program of four R-rated "Fairytale Fantasies." Commonwealth continued to list the Zuni among its holdings in the annual *Motion Picture Almanac* through the 1985 edition, suggesting that it may have been considering reopening the drive-in, but even that listing ended in 1986.

An elementary school sits where the old concession-projection building had been, but stumps of the old screen tower and overgrown hints of the ramps remain today.

Yucca Drive-In

Opened: Sept. 28, 1951

Closed: July 21, 1958

Capacity: 249 cars

Location: On Route 66 on the west side of town, just east of the airport.

William Nagle and Theatre Enterprises, which ran Gallup's indoor theaters, bought a 10-acre site for the city's first drive-in in the fall of 1949. Construction was delayed, and the start of the Korean War added restrictions on certain materials in theater building. When Nagle finally got a drive-in permit from the National Production Authority in the summer of 1951, his project was to be called the Gallup Drive-In. When it opened, it had been renamed the Yucca. Its relatively small screen was supported by five poles 46 feet high.

The Yucca's grand opening went well, but rain later that night canceled the following performance. Manager Bruce Waugh said the next day that the drive-in's long access road from 66 hadn't been surfaced yet, so it would be "too rough for an audience this evening."

The Yucca still appeared to be in the middle of nowhere in this USGS aerial photo, taken in Sept. 1952, a year after the drive-in opened.

By 1957, Nagle was in charge of Gallup's movie houses for Frontier Theatres, which turned its attention to the larger, newer Zuni on the other side of town. Immediately, the Yucca became the second-best drive-in in town, with older films at a cheaper price. That arrangement lasted less than a year; in July 1958, the Yucca's ad in the *Gallup Daily Independent* abruptly announced that it would close for the season. It never reopened. A grocery store and its parking lot occupy the site today.

Top and bottom of the ad in the *Gallup Daily Independent* that said the Yucca Drive-In would close for the 1958 season on a Monday in July.

Intermission:
Route 66 Motel Neon

All right, let me tell you how this intermission is on theme. One of the most notable features of the drive-ins of Route 66 was their neon signs. Dozens of contemporary accounts mention their dazzling signs and screen towers. Sadly, few color photos of that neon survive.

To provide a sense of what those great old signs must have been like, here are a few photos of Route 66 neon signs from the motels of the Mother Road. New Mexico has probably the best collection of them, especially the iconic Blue Swallow Motel of Tucumcari. Enjoy!

The iconic Roy's in Amboy CA.
@ appalachianview | Depositphotos.com

El Trovatore Motel, Kingman AZ.
Photo (cropped for space) by Flickr user Jerry Huddleston.

New Mexico

Circle "S" Motel, Tucumcari NM. Circa 1960 postcard, Newberry Library, James R. Powell Route 66 Postcard Collection.

Desert Hills Motel, Tulsa OK. © Yaniv Adir | Dreamstime.com

Rest Haven Court, Lebanon MO. © Steve Lagreca | Dreamstime.com

Munger Moss Motel, Lebanon MO. 2009 photo from Carol M. Highsmith's America, Library of Congress, Prints and Photographs Division.

El Vado Motel, Albuquerque NM. 2020 photo from Carol M. Highsmith's America, Library of Congress, Prints and Photographs Division.

Monterey Motel, Albuquerque NM. 2020 photo from Carol M. Highsmith's America, Library of Congress, Prints and Photographs Division.

New Mexico

Nob Hill Court, formerly the Modern Auto Court and the Nob Hill Motel, Albuquerque NM. 2020 photo from Carol M. Highsmith's America, Library of Congress, Prints and Photographs Division.

De Anza Motor Lodge, Albuquerque NM. 2020 photo from Carol M. Highsmith's America, Library of Congress, Prints and Photographs Division.

Wigwam Motel, Holbrook AZ. More about it in the next intermission. 2006 photo from Carol M. Highsmith's America, Library of Congress, Prints and Photographs Division.

Supai Motel, Seligman AZ. 2016 photo from Carol M. Highsmith's America, Library of Congress, Prints and Photographs Division.

El Rancho Hotel & Motel, Gallup NM. Photo (cropped for space) by Flickr user Nicholas Jones.

The Blue Swallow Motel, Tucumcari NM, is arguably the best place to take a Route 66 motel neon photo. I looked through dozens of them, and my favorite is this one (cropped for space) by Flickr user Harry Pherson.

Arizona

If you saw the movie *Cars*, you saw a lot of magnificent striped, rocky backgrounds that look a lot like Arizona. The state has miles of glorious scenery, but not a lot of drive-ins. My guess is that's because summers can get pretty hot there.

Holbrook

When I think of Holbrook, at least three Route 66 icons come to mind. Joe & Aggie's Café, which opened in 1946, closed during the pandemic and may not reopen. The Wigwam Motel, built in 1950 and now listed in the National Register of Historic Places, still offers a great place to spend the night. And Holbrook is the closest city to the Petrified Forest, the only national park with 66 running through it.

Western Star Drive-In

Opened: March 19, 1955

Closed: May? 1955

Capacity: 200 cars

Location: Just east of Route 66 about 1½ miles northeast of town.

On the far west side of Colorado near Dove Creek, Elizabeth Young and her son Robert, both from just across the border in Utah, built the tiny Auto-Vu Drive-In in 1953. It held only about 130 cars. The drive-in probably did really well or not well enough, because in the winter of 1954-55, Robert moved to Holbrook to build the Western Star. (**Crossover alert:** The full story of the Auto-Vu is in my 2020 book *Drive-Ins of Colorado*.)

Young started with a small drive-in in Holbrook, although larger than the one he left behind. He told the *Holbrook Tribune News* that he could expand it to 500 cars if there was enough demand. The Western Star had a wide screen and a "big neon sign" by its driveway on 66. The drive-in opened right after the car speakers arrived from Denver.

The owners of Holbrook's indoor Roxy Theatre moved quickly to open their own drive-in a month later (see below). Against that competition, the Western Star floundered almost immediately. Young discontinued the drive-in's family night in late April "due to overhead expenses," and his May 13 ad pleaded "This is your home-owned Drive-In – Your Patronage will help our town grow." That was the final movie ad for Holbrook's Western Star, although it sponsored a turkey shoot on May 28. Nothing remains of the drive-in; Lisitzky Park's athletic fields occupy the site today.

There's a little bit of a happy ending for the Youngs. Right after the drive-in closed, Robert and his wife moved to Buckeye AZ, about 25 miles west of Phoenix. They quickly built another Western Star Drive-In there, opening on Aug.

The Western Star's grand opening ad from the *Holbrook Tribune-News*.

26, 1955. The new drive-in also had 200 speakers and room to grow, and its wide screen was 85x40 feet. I would bet that the neon sign, the speakers, and maybe even the screen made the trip with the Youngs as they left Holbrook. In early 1957, a windstorm blew down the new Western Star's screen, and that's when the Youngs sold out to the Louis Long company, which owned Buckeye's indoor Roxy Theatre.

66 Drive-In

Opened: April 17, 1955

Closed: Aug. 16, 1957

Capacity: 400 cars

Location: On the west side of Route 66 about one mile northeast of town.

The Harry Nace Theatre company was a very big deal in Arizona. It owned dozens of theaters, including Holbrook's indoor Roxy, which it moved to a new building in 1954. Nace probably didn't relish the prospect of a competitor, and it rushed the construction of its own drive-in about 2000 feet closer to town than the Western Star's sign on the opposite side of the street. The 66 opened four weeks after its rival, boasting "the largest screen in Eastern Arizona and the third largest in the state."

Whether it was the chain's modern setting, with

The 66's ramps and concession stand survived for years, as shown in this 1964 USGS photo.

a playground and cafeteria-style concession stand, its access to fresher movies, or even the fact that anyone driving to the Western Star had to pass the 66's marquee, Nace's drive-in quickly buried its competitor. Maybe that was the plan; just a few weeks after the Western Star closed, the 66 reduced its schedule to four days a week.

By the summer of 1957, the statewide Nace movie ad in the *Arizona Republic* had dropped the 66 from its list. The drive-in's final ad in the *Holbrook Tribune-News* was on August 16 that year. Two weeks later, ads for the Roxy continued, but the 66 was gone. The screen and viewing field lingered through at least 1959, and Nace included it in its annual list of theaters through 1961, but the 66 apparently never reopened. The Roxy is still active under new ownership, but nothing remains of the drive-in today. A Dollar General store sits about where the 66's entrance had been.

Winslow

Sure, everyone thinks of the Eagles' song "Take It Easy," (written by Jackson Browne), which the city has embraced with a "Standin' on the Corner" park downtown. My favorite place in town is a few blocks east. La Posada Hotel, a former Harvey House, includes a museum, art gallery, and gardens. It's an oasis in the desert next to an active Amtrak stop.

Tonto Drive-In

Opened: Oct. 12, 1951

Closed: Sept. 12, 1985

Capacity: 300 cars

Location: On Route 66 about 1½ miles west of town.

In 2000, 15 years after the Tonto closed, the screen, concession stand, ramps, and speaker poles still looked ready to show a movie. [Drive-In Theater, Winslow, Arizona]. NAU.PH.2013.4.1.10.18.32. Running, John. Special Collections and Archives, Cline Library, Northern Arizona University.

Winslow mayor F. C. Whipple turned the first shovel of earth in the Tonto's ground-breaking ceremony on Aug. 31, 1951. That the drive-in opened just six weeks later showed the efficiency of its owner, Harry Nace, Arizona movie magnate. It was originally planned for 500 cars, but Nace settled for 300 with room to expand.

When it opened, the Tonto's 60x55-foot screen, covered with an asbestos reflecting surface, faced a graveled lot and a 36x40-foot projection-concession building. The drive-in's location next to a busy railroad almost guaranteed at least one passing train per movie. One of the opening night movies was *Return of the Frontiersman*, which starred Julie London, who later married Bobby Troup, who wrote the iconic "Route 66" song.

In 1955, Winslow almost got a second Nace drive-in, south of the tracks near the airport. The city council

By 2019, pretty much all that was left of the Tonto was the husk of the sign. Photo by the author.

granted a lease in May that year, and construction started in June. Enough citizens objected to the city council's move, mostly on traffic worries about the railroad crossing bottleneck, that the council exercised a short-term cancellation clause in the lease in July, one day before Nace's contractor was to pour concrete for the foundation.

Meanwhile, the Tonto persevered. By 1977, with the closing of the indoor Rialto, it was the only active movie theater within 30 miles. In March 1981, wind gusts knocked down the old wooden screen tower, which was replaced with an 80x40-foot steel structure in May. The Tonto closed after the 1985 season, though it never completely went away. The screen lasted long enough for Oliver Stone to use it as a backdrop in his 1993 movie *Natural Born Killers*. What's left of the marquee is still there today.

Flagstaff

The Coconino National Forest, which surrounds the city, and the altitude, about 7000 feet, give the Flagstaff an atmosphere unlike the rest of Arizona. It's got a fine visitor center and some classic Route 66 sights, though my favorite place there is the Lowell Observatory, which holds the telescope that Clyde Tombaugh used to discover Pluto in 1930.

Mt. Elden Drive-In

Opened: May 29, 1953

Closed: Oct. 9, 1977

Capacity: 800 cars

Location: On Route 66 about 2½ miles east of Flagstaff.

Harry Nace's company, Northern Arizona Theatres, broke ground on the Mt. Elden in October 1951, just a few days before its Tonto Drive-In opened in Winslow. The work took longer than the Tonto's, possibly reflecting the shorter building season due to Flagstaff's more variable climate. Construction took a break over the winter while Nace gathered supplies, then the work continued so slowly afterward that the grand opening was delayed until spring 1953.

When the Mt. Elden finally opened, it sported a 64x40-foot screen. The snack

This grainy photo of the Mt. Elden sign appeared in its 1958 season opening ad in the *Arizona Daily Sun*.

bar featured views of both the screen and the projection room, where radio station disc jockeys broadcast shows in the evening. Its viewing field held 400 cars with room for expansion, which came in 1957.

That was also the year Flagstaff almost got a second drive-in. Northern Arizona Theatres announced that it had purchased 10 acres of land west of town on US 66. They cleared the field, erected the screen posts and speaker poles, and then unexpectedly stopped.

A few color photos exist of the Mt. Elden's screen and parts of its viewing field, but only behind a motel built years after the drive-in. Aerial: Americana Motel, Mt. Elden Drive In Route 66. NAU.PH.85.3.231.8. Fronske Studio. Special Collections and Archives, Cline Library, Northern Arizona University.

The Mt. Elden lived a quiet life under corporate ownership. Manager Jim King told the Northern Arizona University school newspaper in 1974 that the drive-in was showing mostly reruns, and that it would close by the end of September "because it gets too cold." After the 1977 season, an investment company bought the Mt. Elden and quickly cleared away the screen and the speaker poles, but it sat idle for years. A new post office branch was built there in 1987, and it's still there today.

Kingman

The Mohave Museum in Kingman, in addition to exhibits about Route 66, Native Americans, and mining, has a room dedicated to the city's favorite son, film and TV star Andy Devine. His trademark raspy voice made him the perfect sidekick in a long string of Westerns.

Sage Drive-In

Opened: September 1956

Closed: 1968

Capacity: 400 cars

Location: On Route 66 about a mile east of town.

Although Harry Nace had owned the local Lang Theatre Company since 1939, he formed a new corporation in 1955, Westside Theatres, to build a drive-in Kingman as well as drive-ins in Goodyear, Litchfield, Scottsdale, and Tempe. The first mention of the Sage in Nace's statewide listings in the *Arizona Republic* came on Sept. 14, 1956, although the drive-in may have opened a few days earlier.

I'll admit it. I couldn't find any local resources for the fairly short history of the Sage. In April 1957, strong winds knocked down the screen, which fell on a power line and knocked out service nearby. In 1968, the Arizona Highway Department contracted Fronske Studios to take property condemnation photos for US 66 businesses that were going to have to make way for I-40. That's how I know the drive-in had a glorious sign that read "The Sage."

The drive-in didn't reopen in 1969. In its place,

In 1968, the state highway department commissioned a series of US 66 right-of-way photos including this one of the Sage's sign. Kingman, 1968. [The Sage Drive in Theater.] NAU.PH.85.3.231.8. Fronske Studio. Special Collections and Archives, Cline Library, Northern Arizona University.

the highway department built an oval off-ramp from I-40 to what became old US 66, or state highway 66, or Andy Devine Avenue. The Sage's viewing field was faintly visible for years, but today it's just a flat oval.

Intermission:
Wigwam Motels

As we cross from Arizona to California, one Route 66 legacy that the two states share is the Wigwam Motel. The concrete teepees were undoubtedly the inspiration for the Cozy Cone Motel in *Cars'* Radiator Springs. Two of the three surviving examples of this unusual tourist stop are on the Mother Road. One is in Holbrook AZ, the other in San Bernardino CA. I've stayed in them both.

First, some history. In 1933, Frank Redford built a court of teepee-shaped motel cabins, which he called a Wigwam Village, around a Native American artifact museum in Horse Cave KY. He got a design patent for the buildings' in 1936. The second Wigwam Village went up just a few miles down US 31W in Cave City the following year, and still exists today.

Of the three surviving Wigwam Motels, only the one in Cave City KY has this interesting neon triangle. © Sequential5 | Dreamstime.com

In 1950, when this postcard was published, Holbrook's Wigwam Village included a gas station. From the Newberry Library's James R. Powell Route 66 Postcard Collection.

The third, fourth, and fifth Wigwam Villages were built in the 1940s in New Orleans LA, Orlando FL, and Bessemer AL. They've all been demolished. Charles Lewis built "Number 6" in Holbrook in 1950 after licensing Redford's patent. He laid out the 15 teepees on three sides of a rectangle. The main office sits in a regular building in the center. Originally, there had been a gas station near the office.

Lewis closed the village in 1974. He passed away in 1986, then his sons Clifton and Paul Lewis renovated the place and reopened in 1988. It's been listed in the National Register of Historic Places since 2002.

Redford built the westernmost Wigwam Village in the late 1940s, barely east of Rialto. I don't know why it's "Number 7" even though it was built before Holbrook's. Redford put 19 units on either side of an arc of pavement with a small swimming pool at the center. It was added to the National Register of Historic Places in 2012.

San Bernardino's Wigwam still looks a lot like its 1977 photo. John Margolies Roadside America photograph archive (1972-2008), Library of Congress, Prints and Photographs Division.

Let me tell you what I saw when I slept in a Wigwam, twice. Each 32-foot-high unit has a diameter of 14 feet at the base. Inside, there's a decent-sized motel room with a bed or two, cable TV, and an air conditioner mounted in the window. Behind the room is a very small bathroom with a shower. To me, the unusual tilt of the wall was most obvious in the shower, but it's quite usable. Parking is right at the front door at both locations.

Holbrook's Wigwam room felt like a time capsule of a 1960s motel. The TV was an old cathode ray tube type, and the lighting came from floor and table lamps. San Bernardino's was just as retro on the outside, but the inside felt much closer to a modern motel room with a flat-screen TV, wall-mounted lighting, and a sofa. In both places, neighboring guests were friendly; they too were traveling Route 66. Then when I went inside, the room was surprisingly quiet. (My Holbrook teepee was away from the railroad tracks, closer to the quiet street.) Maybe thick concrete makes for good sound insulation.

For the full Route 66 experience, I recommend you stay at either of the clean, moderately priced Wigwam Motels on the highway. If you can, try them both.

California

California is huge, so there were plenty of drive-ins there. Southern California had mostly great weather and a lot of residents, so their drive-ins were also huge. Among US states, only Texas could hold more total cars in its drive-ins than California.
But Route 66 didn't pass by very many of them because it ran just one thin stripe across the narrow state. The Mother Road's lonely path through the Mojave Desert between Needles and Barstow is the longest stretch between drive-ins anywhere on 66.

Needles

The Atchison, Topeka, and Santa Fe Railroad built a landmark to replace the Needles depot that burned in 1906. The El Garces was a glorious Harvey House, providing an oasis of Classical Revival style in the desert. At press time, the city was renovating the place with plans to open it as a hotel and a Route 66 museum.

Sands Drive-In

Opened: July 31, 1953

Closed: Oct. 15, 1953

Capacity: 270 cars

Location: On Route 66 just west of town.

The only known picture of the Sands was in the background of this 1955 image of a flash flood in front of the Ranch House truck stop across the highway. Photo by Elmer Kramer, used by permission.

The Western Amusement Company owned dozens of movie houses, most of them indoors, including the Needles Theater. Western spent more time planning the city's drive-in theater than operating it. In April 1952, local Western manager Edward "E. R." Crouch told the city's chamber of commerce that the company was planning to build a drive-in to the west of the city limits.

A formal announcement followed in January 1953, noting that a 60x40-foot screen would face 400 cars. In early July, Crouch held a naming contest, offering a full year's pass for the winner. On opening day, "the most modern theatre in the Colorado River Valley" saw attendants directing cars to any of 270 parking spots.

An important fact that might not have occurred to Western executives is that, in the summer, Needles is hot. Really hot. For example, the city hit 125 degrees in both 2005 and 2016. To put that in perspective, noted hot spot Las Vegas NV's all-time high is 117. Weather records indicated that August and September 1953 were normal for Needles, with triple-digit highs almost every afternoon. The temperature falls quickly in the desert at night, but not quickly enough to make an early evening show a pleasant experience.

The final ad for the Sands in the *Needles Desert Star* came on Oct. 8, listing movies through Oct. 15. Crouch transferred to Oregon in February, and the Sands was rarely mentioned again, although it stayed intact for quite a while. In 1966, after a dozen idle years, the Sands projection room still held some $5,000 worth of equipment, which it lost to burglars that summer.

The Sands viewing field was flattened a decade later, and a truck parking lot occupies the site today. It's behind a small truck stop that features a statue of Spike, Snoopy's brother in the comic strip *Peanuts*. Spike's hometown is Needles.

Barstow

Barstow grew up as a crossroads even before Route 66 arrived. The Casa del Desierto hotel-train station, another Harvey House, opened in 1911 and now houses the Mother Road Museum. A fake train station on the east side of town was called the world's largest McDonalds when it opened in 1975. Since there's an adjacent bus station, it's also sometimes called the world's busiest McDonalds.

Skyline Drive-In

Opened: Sept. 30, 1966

~~Closed:~~ ~~1988~~ ~~2009~~ ~~2015~~ active

Capacity: 630 cars

Location: On Old Highway 58 about two miles north of Route 66.

Barstow's Skyline may have had more stops and starts than any other drive-in. Western Amusement, which ran the other theaters in Barstow, announced in early 1953 that it would build a 650-car drive-in and had already ordered the equipment. In 1955, San Bernardino County approved construction of a proposed 1200-car twin-screen drive-in. Eight years later, in 1963, Western Amusement picked R. Benedict Brout to be the architect of a 600-car drive-in in Barstow.

The Skyline's grand opening ad as it appeared in Barstow's *Desert Dispatch*.

Despite all of these announcements and unexplained delays, Western Amusement didn't open the Skyline until late 1966, with a single 90x60-foot screen. After all those false starts, the drive-in settled down for a couple of decades of quiet corporate ownership. In the spring of 1988, the Skyline was slow to reopen as the manager complained about vandalism and ramp repairs. The drive-in reopened for a couple of months near the end of that year, then stayed closed.

In 1994, drive-in movie critic Joe Bob Briggs noticed a "For Sale or Lease" sign in front of the Skyline. The next year, serial drive-in entrepreneur Larry Rodkey low-balled an offer and added it to his handful of theaters. After months of renovation, Rodkey reopened the Skyline in July 1996. Business was so good that in 1999, Rodkey bought the damaged screen from an Antioch CA drive-in, trimming it to a clean 45x35 feet to use as the Skyline's second screen.

The Skyline doesn't have its name on its sign, and the top part, now blank, used to advertise a weekend swap meet. You can barely see the smaller, second screen behind the sign. 2019 photo by the author.

Rodkey operated the drive-in for about 10 years, then leased it to manager Randy Shull. After a couple of years, Shull shut down the Skyline in August 2009. Two months later, Gene Harvey took over the lease and reopened.

When the movie studios began requiring digital projectors, Harvey tried and failed to win one in a national contest sponsored by Honda. He closed the Skyline in February 2015. Rodkey came to the rescue, spending more for two new projectors than he had spent for the entire drive-in 20 years earlier. The Skyline reopened yet again in April 2015, and it's still going strong today.

Lenwood

In 1923, Frank and Ellen Woods owned about 1500 acres of desert. They whipped up a deal to subdivide it into Lenwood Estates, named for the wife and run by William Barnard. According to a 1927 California Supreme Court ruling, "The whole scheme was from its inception one to cheat and defraud," which sounds harsh. Today this Barstow suburb is a census-designated place of about 1100 households.

Bar-Len Drive-In

Opened: Dec. 29, 1948

Closed: Sept. 15, 1968

Capacity: 400 cars

Location: At the southwest corner of Lenwood on Route 66.

When this picture appeared as part of an ad in the 1963 Barstow High School yearbook, *El Desierto*, it was reversed. Flipping it, as shown above, points the screen correctly, northeast toward Barstow, with US 66 in the background.

Teenager Janice Wise poses in front of the Bar-Len marquee in this 1954 photo by her sister, Judy Wise. Used by permission.

Patrick "P. K." Lyons got a construction permit in the fall of 1948 to build the area's first drive-in. The Bar-Len opened just before the end of the year, already outfitted with a snack bar and in-car speakers and heaters. The 72x68-foot screen tower supported a 50x45-foot screen facing a 10-acre lot. The drive-in was probably busy; in June 1949 it offered a service for "elderly patrons" in which an attendant would park their car at a ramp for them.

Western Amusement Company, which ran Barstow's indoor theaters, acquired the Bar-Len in 1951. The company would often show a film at the Forum or the Barstow theaters, then show it again with a second feature at the drive-in.

Of course, the Bar-Len took its name from its position near the border of Barstow and Lenwood, but the presence or absence of a hyphen in the drive-in's correct spelling is an enduring question. Many references, and possibly its street sign, presented the name as two words. A surviving intermission trailer, plus most of its newspaper ads, included the hyphen.

After the more modern Skyline opened in late 1966 on the opposite end of Barstow, Western probably concluded that the area couldn't support two drive-ins. The Bar-Len posted a "Closed for the winter" ad after the 1968 season, but never reopened. Lenwood Road now cuts through the old viewing field, though traces of ramps are still visible amid the desert scrub.

Victorville

Victorville started in the 19th century as a miners' supply town, and the arid climate helped preserve its buildings even when the boom petered out. After the turn of the century, the town's authentic look and proximity to Hollywood attracted the film industry, which shot over 200 westerns there. Today it's the home of the California Route 66 Museum.

Joshua Drive-In

Opened: May 29, 1953

Closed: Dec. 29, 1982

Capacity: 400 cars

Location: Next to Route 66 almost two miles southwest of town on 7th Street.

In 1947, Jack Baldock moved to California as Western Amusement Co. began a whirlwind of theater construction and acquisition. He bought a piece of two indoor theaters in Victorville that year. In 1950, Western built a third indoor theater for the city, and in October that year, announced that it would build a 600-car drive-in there.

The Joshua's sign hung around for a few years after the drive-in closed, but it's long gone now. Circa 1990 photo by John Gateley, used by permission.

There were delays. The Korean War led to restrictions on building theaters for the next couple of years. In the summer of 1952, four grade-school boys broke into a theater building and vandalized the audio equipment Western Amusement had storing there for the drive-in project. Construction began in earnest in 1953, and the Joshua opened on the last Friday in May with a 400-car viewing field.

After spending a few years running the Centennial Drive-In in Littleton CO, Baldock moved back to Victorville in 1960 to be closer to his theaters. Before and after his arrival, the Joshua lived the relatively quiet life that came with corporate ownership. By the early 1970s, Baldock and Western Amusement were preparing for change. In 1972, they got permission to build a second

Victorville drive-in (see below), and they asked to change the Joshua's zoning to commercial in 1974. It remained the city's only drive-in until the summer of 1981.

In December 1982, Entertainment Centers of America bought all of Western Amusement's Victorville theaters. They ran the Joshua for only about a week, closing for the season just before the New Year and never reopening. Fire destroyed the concession building in December 1988, and bulldozers took down the screen the following March. An appliance store occupies the site today.

Bonus: Balsam Drive-In

Opened: July 1, 1981

Closed: Dec. 28, 1987

Capacity: 510 cars

Location: On Balsam Avenue north of Bear Valley Road, less than a mile east of Route 66. Although its first screen was up before the 66 signs came down, by the time this drive-in finally opened, those signs were long gone. That was close enough for the first edition of this book, but now I don't think it really qualifies.

In late 1972, the San Bernardino County planners approved Western Amusement's planned 625-car drive-in. The company broke ground on the project in November 1973. Mrs. Ted Jones, the founder's widow, said that the city's Joshua Drive-In was too far out of town, and that the newer drive-in would be better positioned "to serve the expanding population of the high desert."

There were delays. By 1974, Western Amusement had built the screen, but it couldn't get water service. The site was between water districts, and Victorville didn't want to extend its pipes to avoid reducing the water

Speaker pole stubs still poked from the sloped hills of the Balsam's old ramps in 2019. Photo by the author.

pressure of the nearby housing development. The districts weren't required to add the drive-in to their service areas, so they declined.

Years later, something changed. Construction restarted in April 1981. The scope of the project expanded to add a second screen to the original. When it opened, just inside the Victorville city limits, the Balsam I & II consisted of two fields holding 255 cars each. Polecat AM radio sound alternated with in-car speakers on the poles.

After all that trouble getting started, the Balsam had a short life. Western Amusement sold it with the rest of its Victorville holdings to Entertainment Centers of America in December 1982. Cinemark later took over the Balsam's operation, and that was the company that closed it near the end of 1987. This time there was no pretense of reopening in the spring; its manager said the drive-in didn't do enough business over the winter to justify maintaining the lease. The property soon went up for sale. At last check, it was still for sale. Stubs of many of the Balsam's speaker poles remain today, poking out from the remains of the paved ramps.

San Bernardino

Route 66 fans can find all sorts of attractions in San Bernardino. It hosts the annual Route 66 Rendezvous, which the city calls the largest classic car show in America. The first McDonalds restaurant is open as a museum. My favorite attraction is the classic Wigwam Motel, which has well-maintained concrete cabins on the outside and modern furnishings in each room.

Mt. Vernon Drive-In

Opened: Sept. 25, 1948

Closed: Sept. 10, 1989

Capacity: 580 cars

Location: On Mt. Vernon Avenue about 1¼ miles south of Business Route 66.

Byron "Bud" Congdon commissioned Drive-In Theatres of America to build one of its patented double-ramp theaters in San Bernardino. When it opened, the Mt. Vernon Motor-In boasted "a natural stage," whatever that looked like.

Congdon soon recognized the value of children in the audience. In late 1950, he instituted a "Family Hour" so that early arrivals paid a lower carload price to get in. (Presumably they would have more time to spend at the concession stand.) In May 1951, the Mt. Vernon

A *Boxoffice* feature hailed the Mt. Vernon's swimming pool as a way for drive-ins to earn money during the day.

The original Mt. Vernon sign was a skinny tower, but Pacific Drive-Ins replaced it with something more modern. 1978 photo © Elisa Leonelli, used by permission.

added a new playground, including a sliding board, tetherballs, and swings, all on a base of 100 tons of sand.

The really big innovation came in 1953, when Congdon built a 105x35-foot swimming pool between the concession stand and the screen. The Cinema-Surf Club also featured a barbecue pit, a lanai, cabanas, and a bathhouse near the pool. Members were able to swim all day, and if they wanted to watch the movie, the pool was open until dark.

The Mt. Vernon Motor-In rolled along until November 1972, when it was bought by Pacific Drive-In Theatres. Not only did Pacific get rid of the swimming pool, they tore up the whole lot, turned it into a two-screener, and reopened in April 1973 as the Mt. Vernon Twin Drive-In. This new version lasted until the end of the 1989 season. The drive-in was razed, then a swap meet popped up on the site's concrete parking lot in 2002. The swap meet closed in October 2021.

Rialto

Route 66 was known as Foothill Boulevard as it passed through Rialto. Fewer than 3500 people lived there when drive-ins sprang up along the Mother Road; over 100,000 people live in Rialto today. The most popular Rialto landmark isn't in Rialto; the Wigwam Motel is served by the Rialto post office but sits just across the border in San Bernardino.

Foothill Drive-In

Opened: March 6, 1948

Closed: Sept. 5, 1988

Capacity: 675 cars

Location: Directly south of Route 66 with an entrance on Eucalyptus Avenue.

William Tharp accomplished a lot in his life. He taught industrial arts in Indiana, where he fathered award-winning choreographer Twyla Tharp. After moving to California after the war, he owned car dealerships and formed a company around his patented lighting design. What we really care about is that he also built the Foothill Drive-In amid the orange orchards next to Route 66.

The Moonlight Movies System was Tharp's system of drive-in parkway and aisle design, of which the Foothill was the first example. His company offered to lease the patent to other drive-in builders. Meanwhile, a storm blew down part of the Foothill's marquee in January 1949, which Tharp repaired. The following March, he added 250 car heaters.

The first serious problem occurred in November 1953. During a movie, two teenagers with a grudge against Tharp poured gasoline on the storage building at the back of the screen tower and lit it with flaming rags. Patrons said the resulting burst of fire looked like an explosion.

The Foothill's grand opening was delayed from earlier in the week. Maybe that's why its first ad in the *San Bernardino County Sun* was so subdued.

The flames warped the tower's steel supports, but no one was hurt. The storage building and its contents were a complete loss, with total damages near $10,000.

Reports suggest that Mrs. Tharp handled most of the day-to-day drive-in operation, with help from Twyla and her brothers, while William spent time adding a gas station and a restaurant to his Rialto empire. By 1971, the Tharps may have begun to lose interest in running the Foothill, leaving it closed for several weeks while they went on vacation. In 1972, Pacific Drive-In Theatres acquired the drive-in, and it ran it quietly from then on. Pacific declined to renew the lease after the 1988 season. A large grocery store occupies the site today.

Fontana

Henry Kaiser built the West Coast's first steel plant in Fontana in 1943. He later founded Kaiser Permanente to provide healthcare for his workers. Before World War II, Fontana was known for its citrus production, selling some of its fresh orange juice from orange-shaped kiosks along the highway. One of the last of these, now called Bono's Historic Orange, sits in the parking lot at Bono's Restaurant there.

Bel-Air Drive-In

Opened: Nov. 21, 1956

Closed: Sept. 10, 1989

Capacity: 1050 cars

Location: About 2.6 miles south of Route 66, just west of Citrus Avenue.

After over a decade as a sales manager for Universal Pictures, Al O'Keefe shifted in 1953 to become a vice-president at Pola-Lite, a 3-D movie equipment company. In 1954, he founded Parliament Pictures, which imported a couple of movies from the UK. Not long after, he joined Ted Gamble's west coast theater circuit. As O'Keefe and Associates, he hired Walter Long to carve out room for a drive-in in the orchards west of Fontana.

The Bel-Air (spelled variously as Belair, Bellaire, or Bel Aire) reportedly cost $350,000 to build and outfit, including a 10-story-high curved screen and a modern cafeteria-style concession stand. Its manager was Joe Greene, who had acted in a few dozen westerns and was

The grand opening ad for the Bel-Air (or Belair?) as it appeared in the *San Bernardino County Sun.*

best known for playing the sheriff in Hopalong Cassidy movies.

The drive-in's opening was delayed by a court battle it initiated over access to first-run movies. In late 1961, almost five years after that lawsuit was filed, a jury ruled against Beacon Theatres, then listed as the Bel-Air's owner, and in favor of Pacific Drive-In Theatres, two other theater chains, and five distributors. Pacific took over the Bel-Air on Jan. 3, 1962, as Beacon agreed to dismiss that chain from its appeal of the jury verdict.

Pacific held on to the Bel-Air for most of three decades, closing on the Sunday after Labor Day, 1989. The screen stayed up for a few more years before being demolished in 1998. A huge indoor auto parts facility occupies the site today.

Montclair

Route 66 didn't go through Montclair. It followed Foothill Boulevard through Upland, immediately north of Montclair. But one of the city's drive-ins was just close enough to the Mother Road to merit inclusion in this list. The other, which opened in 1956 as the Mission, is still active. Although it announced in November 2019 that it would soon close, the Mission Tiki saw a new surge of business after Covid, and now shows no sign of closing.

Valley Drive-In

Opened: April 14, 1948

Closed: Sept. 13, 1977

Capacity: 650 cars

Location: Almost three miles south of Route 66 on Central Avenue.

The Valley's elaborate neon mural stayed intact through the entire life of the drive-in. 1978 photo © Elisa Leonelli, used by permission.

Arnold and Jack Anderson, who operated a few indoor theaters in the area, started building the Valley in early 1948. They were part of Sero Enterprises, run by William Oldknow, and Sero was listed as the drive-in's owner for all of its life. In turn, Sero somehow cooperated with Pacific Drive-Ins for advertising and probably some other stuff. I find it all too tangled to sort out.

Anyway, the owners weren't the stars of the Valley. That honor falls to the men who designed and created an amazing mural of the Santa Barbara Mission on its 72-foot screen tower. Cal Tyler painted the mural; Ontario Neon, run by Chet Wilkins, connected 2500 feet of multicolored tubing to complement its figures. In the mural's foreground, two oxen pulled a simple cart in front of a priest holding a Bible stamped with a blue-neon cross. There were mountains in the background, the Spanish mission, and a clump of cactus in the corner. Wilkins assembled it in the basement of the First Baptist Church in Ontario CA because its floor was large enough to hold it all.

The Valley's marquee in 1948, uploaded by user dallasmovietheaters at CinemaTreasures.org.

When the Valley opened, its screen was 39x55 feet. It offered 300 seats for walk-in patrons, a snack bar, and a children's playground. The Valley's attendants fixed flat tires for free and sold gasoline. In March 1954, it widened its screen to 42x104 feet and became the first drive-in to show a CinemaScope film, with the stereo soundtrack mixed down to a mono feed for the in-car speakers.

In summary, the Valley had 30 seasons of quiet, corporate ownership, with one exception. Burglars pulled off an ingenious heist there in December 1963, covering floors and concrete walks with popcorn kernels so they could roll away its 350-pound safe. The drive-in closed after the 1977 season, and the gorgeous mural was bulldozed in 1980 to be replaced by a car lot. They're still selling cars there today.

La Verne

In La Verne, there's a vintage McDonalds restaurant, designed in 1952, with the first set of golden arches. The classic 1967 film, *The Graduate*, used the United Methodist Church of La Verne to film its wedding scene. In 1993, *Wayne's World 2* returned to the same church for a similar wedding scene.

Mt. Baldy Drive-In

Opened: June 8, 1960

Closed: Jan. 5, 1984

Capacity: 1200 cars

Location: A couple of blocks south of Route 66 at the Fruit Street / White Avenue interchange.

Even though it was built later than most of the drive-ins in this book, my information about the Mt. Baldy is a little fuzzy. First example: Walter G. Long & Associates built the drive-in for $30,000, but were they the owners or just the construction company? Anyway, the Mt. Baldy covered 15 acres and had a huge 100x70-foot screen and a full children's playground. The skiers on its neon sign would light up in sequence as if sliding toward the entrance.

The drive-in's owners, whoever they were, asked the local planning commission in September 1960 to let them build a golf course, driving range, and mini-golf course surrounding the Mt. Baldy. That didn't happen.

Second example: In the summer of 1961, National Theatres and Television bought the drive-in, but the local papers said that Fox West Coast was leasing it and that Cecil Carlton would continue to manage it. In 1966, *Boxoffice* wrote that the Mt. Baldy was one of a chain of theaters Carlton operated, but Fox West Coast's theater list in the *Motion Picture Almanac* continued to include it. Maybe Carlton was at least part-owner?

National General, Fox West Coast's parent company, included the Mt. Baldy in its 1970-72 *MPA* lists. Mann Theatres bought National General in 1973, and was listed in the *MPA* as the drive-in's owner through 1982.

California 249

Reportedly, this elaborate sign is in storage somewhere, waiting to be restored. 1977 photo by John Margolies, Roadside America photograph archive (1972-2008), Library of Congress, Prints and Photographs Division.

Third example: In 1977, John Forte, manager of the Mt. Baldy, got the city council to okay a second screen for his drive-in, although there's no evidence that the second screen was ever built. Was that the same John Forte who owned the Santee Drive-In in San Diego?

The *MPA*, often slow to react to changes, began listing Larry Jacobs as the Mt. Baldy's owner in its 1983 edition, so the transition might have been years earlier. Jacobs' 1990 obituary confirmed that he had owned it as well as the Eagle Theatre in Eagle Rock CA. At least everyone seems to agree that the drive-in closed in 1984.

In addition to its skier sign, the Mt. Baldy had a smaller neon sign directing visitors to the Los Angeles County Fairgrounds. The fair restored that smaller sign and reinstalled it just east of the Fairplex's Gate 15 in 2008. They're reported to have the larger sign in storage, waiting for restoration funding. Today, White Avenue crosses the site of the drive-in's old viewing field, and a post office building has replaced the screen.

Azusa

The city of Azusa is known for two things, maybe three. Its Spanish Revival styled Civic Center, completed in 1928 and expanded in 1945, is in the National Register of Historic Places. Azusa Pacific is a Christian university on Route 66; Azusa's drive-in site is now part of its campus, and its neon sign remains a Mother Road landmark.

Azusa Foothill Drive-In

Opened: Dec. 20, 1961

Closed: Dec. 29, 2001

Capacity: 1510 cars

Location: On the north side of Route 66 where it joins Foothill Boulevard.

Edwards Theatres built the Azusa Foothill on a former orange grove, adding it to a drive-in roster that included the Edwards, the San Gabriel, and the Sunland. A long driveway lined with trees and gooseneck streetlamps led from the highway to the ticket booth.

Azusa Pacific University restored and maintains the Foothill marquee on old Route 66. I hear that it looks really nice at night. Photo by Bill Eichelberger, used by permission.

In its 40 years of corporate ownership, the drive-in had at least a few notable events. In 1969, a windstorm knocked the lights out during a performance and tore panels off the screen. During a showing of *Planet of the Apes*, a guy in a gorilla suit jumped on patrons' cars. Eleven gang members were arrested at the drive-in one night in 1992 after violence broke out during a showing of *American Me*. In 2000, the climax of the movie *Psycho Beach Party*, shot on the site, included a climb up the Asuza Foothill screen.

Neighboring Azusa Pacific University bought the drive-in's 19-acre site in 2001 and soon announced plans to demolish it. California's Historical Resources Commission declared the Azusa Foothill an official state landmark in 2002, but the university and the Azusa City Council successfully fought off attempts to preserve it. The screen went down in 2005, and the school converted the field into a parking lot. At least it kept the marquee, renovating and relighting it in October 2007.

Duarte

Duarte started as an orange-growing district over 100 years ago, named for Andres Duarte, the man who built an irrigation ditch to make it possible. (You can find his statue facing Route 66 in Plaza Duarte.) So it's only right that the city's drive-in theater popped up in the middle of an orange grove.

Big Sky Drive-In

Opened: Oct. 20, 1949

Closed: Sept. 9, 1984

Capacity: 850 cars

Location: One block south of Route 66 east of Mountain Avenue.

In 1948, when architect J. Arthur Drielsma was planning the drive-in, it was called the Midway. By the time Lou Berman's group started construction the following spring, the name had changed to Big Sky. For some reason, there were delays that year; the drive-in didn't open until a chilly night in October. A few Hollywood celebrities appeared on the 72-foot stage at the grand opening. The emcee that night was Jack Benny's summer replacement, and future tonight show host, Jack Paar. Other notables included the latest movie actor to star as Tarzan, Lex Barker, and a young comedian named Dick Martin.

Berman seemed enthusiastic for a while, booking an aerial circus act to drum up business for what he advertised as the "World's Largest Theatre Screen." Then In December 1951, Berman sold his share to one of his

Although its screen backed up against Central Avenue, the Big Sky's marquee was right on Route 66. 1978 photo © Elisa Leonelli, used by permission.

partners, former United Artists salesman Jack Drum. Less than two years later, in April 1953, Drum turned the Big Sky over to Bill Katsky. Then in October 1953, Pacific Drive-Ins swooped in to add the drive-in to its Los Angeles-area ozoner empire.

Under corporate ownership, the Big Sky's story got quiet for a few decades. The Southern California Rapid Transit District opened a park-and-ride lot at the drive-in in the summer of 1975. By 1980, the city of Duarte hungered to replace the Big Sky with something that would produce more tax revenue. It couldn't put together enough land for a full-sized enclosed mall, but the city bought the drive-in property for $3.2 million. The result was a small shopping center anchored by a department store, which opened a year after the drive-in closed. Today that store is a Target, and nothing remains of the Big Sky.

Arcadia

There's plenty of art deco architecture left in Arcadia, but my favorite place in town is Santa Anita Park, still racing horses today. The track appeared frequently in TV shows and movies, including the Marx Brothers' *A Day at the Races*, *National Lampoon's Vacation*, two versions of *A Star is Born*, and dozens more.

Edwards Drive-In

Opened: May 6, 1949

Closed: Sept. 10, 1992

Capacity: 750 cars

Location: On Live Oak Avenue and Peck Road, about two miles south of Route 66.

James Edwards II, head of the Edwards Theatres circuit, commissioned architect S. Charles Lee to design his new drive-in. He didn't require city approval because

The Edwards' screen leaned forward a bit, as shown here in a photo from the 1949-50 *Theatre Catalog*.

When the Edwards widened its screen, it kept the lean. Except for the taller palm trees, it looked much the same in 1978 as it did almost 30 years earlier. Photo © Elisa Leonelli, used by permission.

the site was in an unincorporated 16-acre slice of Los Angeles County between Monrovia, Irwindale, and Arcadia. Lee delivered the Edwards Drive-In, which had a 45x67-foot screen that leaned toward the viewing field, providing a better angle for patrons. The screen tower was partly fabricated in Seattle and required special train equipment to ship it to the site.

In February 1954, several trade publications reported that Pacific Theatres had added the Edwards to its regional drive-in empire, but either that didn't happen or Edwards got his drive-in back. Sometime around the late 1950s, the theater expanded with a few more narrow ramps on its north side. The Los Angeles County Medical Association used the drive-in as a polio inoculation site in December 1960.

The Edwards held its first weekend swap meets in 1968, and by 1973 was occasionally dabbling in X-rated movies. In the 1980s, it was the swap meet that got the drive-in in trouble with its neighbors. The weekend sales became so popular that they attracted as many as 10,000 customers a day. Parking became a serious problem, especially for the parishioners of a church across the street. Edwards responded by paying $1.8 million for 9.3 acres, which it converted to a parking lot. He later said that the swap meet was pulling in "far more revenue" than the drive-in.

The Edwards marquee stayed unchanged after the drive-in closed except for slowly losing its letters. Photo posted by user ChrisB at CinemaTreasures.org.

In 1988, the Edwards lost its license to operate the swap meet. The company requested an extension on the license through Nov. 5, 1991, the date the county's permit to operate the drive-in would expire. In November 1990, a fake diner was built at the site for the filming of *There Goes My Baby*, a movie that wasn't released until 1994 because its studio went bankrupt. The 1991 deadline came and went, but the Edwards kept showing movies until the Thursday after Labor Day 1992. The marquee remained standing, losing its "Temporarily Closed" letters a few at a time for several more years. The entire site was converted to a housing development by 2003; nothing remains of the drive-in today.

Pasadena

Pasadena's got a lot going on, with the Rose Bowl, the Jet Propulsion Laboratory, and the Mount Wilson

Observatory just for starters. For Route 66 fans, it's the launching point for the Arroyo Seco Parkway, the area's first freeway. Built in 1940, the parkway is a strange, twisty thrill ride to downtown Los Angeles.

Hastings Drive-In

Opened: May 11, 1950

Closed: Sept. 3, 1968

Capacity: 1315 cars

Location: Less than half a mile north of Route 66 on Rosemead Boulevard.

Comet Theatres, headed by Robert H. Hoese of Salt Lake City, came to the Hastings Ranch area of Pasadena to build the company's first drive-in. Plans for the 12-acre site included a 60-ton screen tower holding a 83½x80-foot screen, a 20x80-foot stage in front, and later a playground and a miniature railroad. The grand opening featured, in person, Roy Rogers, Dale Evans, and Trigger. But the most remarkable part of the Hastings was its marquee.

Not only was the Hastings sign 50 feet high, its attraction board was a translucent panel with slots for 17-inch red and green Bevelite letters. The lights within the panel would cycle from yellow to red, causing the red letters to stand out, then to green, which would do the same for the green letters.

This blurry *Boxoffice* photo gave a hint about how the color-changing Hastings marquee looked at night.

Electrical Products Corp. of Los Angeles called the effect "animated light."

Sometime in the early 1950s, John Danz of Seattle-based Sterling Theatres came along. In 1952, a *Boxoffice* article called him the head of Comet Theatres, and soon Sterling owned the Hastings, occasionally called the Hastings Ranch. On Friday nights in the 1950s, Bill Garr emceed live shows with records and in-person celebrity interviews. One day in 1958, Pasadena firemen had to rescue a teenage painter when winds blew down his ladder as he worked on the top of the Hastings sign.

This construction photo from *Boxoffice* provided a sense of the scale of the Hastings sign as well as a glimpse of the screen.

The drive-in was dismantled in 1968 to make room for the Pasadena Hastings indoor theater, which opened that October. Today, a Trader Joe's sits where the drive-in's screen had stood.

Los Angeles

It's fitting that the home of Hollywood had the earliest drive-in near Route 66. The history of the city's drive-ins is a microcosm of the industry as a whole. It got an early start, added a lot more of them in the postwar boom, then saw them close one by one as urban sprawl made their land irresistible to developers.

Other Los Angeles drive-ins more than three miles from Route 66: Centinela (1950-1993), Electric Dusk (2012-2020, before moving to Glendale), Harbor (1950-1972), Twin-Vue (1949-1981), Victory (1949-1977). Plus many more in various Los Angeles suburbs.

Los Feliz Drive-In

Opened: March 24, 1950

Closed: Oct. 2, 1956

Capacity: 500 cars

Location: Just north of Glendale Avenue where it crosses the Los Angeles River, about 2.7 miles northeast of Route 66 where it turns into Santa Monica Boulevard.

Marvin Chesebro's Los Feliz was an odd little twin-screen, built on land owned by famous shoe designer Frank Sbicca. It had been the home of the Los Angeles Horse Show before Sbicca bought it; the stables, bleachers, and sprinkler system all had to go to make room for the drive-in. Its ads suggested that the Los Feliz

The drawing in the Los Feliz's grand opening ad in the *Highland Park News-Herald* provided a pretty good view of the drive-in's layout.

always showed the same double feature on both of its screens.

Soon after it opened, the drive-in ran into trouble with the bright lights used on a playing field in nearby Griffith Park. Chesebro was an attorney, and he sued to force the city to erect a light shield or stop using the lights. City attorney Ray Chesebro, Marvin's dad, disqualified himself from the case, and the drive-in won its first round in court in June 1950. That preliminary injunction was dissolved in July, and in October a judge ruled that the city lights were there first. Marvin's appeal of the decision never went anywhere.

Somehow the Los Feliz persisted. In 1953, it advertised a new Kiddieland and roof garden. In 1955, *Motion Picture Herald* noted that Claude Ford was operating the drive-in.

In one way, the Los Feliz was ahead of its time. It closed not because it was unpopular but because its land was too valuable – in this case for the Golden State Freeway (I-5), which goes through the site today.

Gilmore Drive-In

Opened: July 18, 1948

Closed: Oct. 31, 1977

Capacity: 650 cars

Location: On 3rd Street east of Fairfax Avenue, about 1.3 miles south of Route 66.

"First the earth cooled. And then the dinosaurs came, but they got too big and fat, so they died and turned to oil." – *Johnny Jacobs, Airplane II: The Sequel*

That's the quote that came to mind as we trace the origin of this drive-in's name. In 1903, farmer Arthur

The Gilmore's marquee, opposite its screen tower, jutted out to the street corner of 3rd & Fairfax. 1976 photo © Elisa Leonelli, used by permission.

Gilmore was drilling for water on his dairy farm and hit oil instead. He formed the Gilmore Oil Company, and his son Earl Bell Gilmore established over 3000 gas stations on the west coast. Their home property was called Gilmore Island, where they built a farmers' market (still operating today) in 1934 and minor-league baseball's Gilmore Field in 1939.

When Sero Enterprises built its drive-in, designed by William Glenn Balch, on the vacant land south of the ballpark and east of the market, of course it used the name Gilmore. The new drive-in had seats for 600 walk-in patrons, though they were often used by teenagers who didn't want to watch movies with their parents. Its marquee façade facing a street corner had a lit signboard jutting out holding movable lettering on three sides.

Within a couple of months, the Gilmore noticed that night games at Gilmore Field meant light pollution for

The Gilmore's impressive screen tower and façade lingered for years after the drive-in closed. 1978 photo © Elisa Leonelli, used by permission.

drive-in patrons, but the place remained popular. For a while, Pacific Theatres took over operation of the Gilmore, using it for the 1954 west coast drive-in debut of the CinemaScope film *The Robe*. At the time, the studio, 20th Century Fox, required stereo sound to go with the wider film format. Rather than buy all new multi-horn speakers, the Gilmore used the wiring of the speaker post lights to add a second set of standard, single-sound speakers.

Sero regained control of the Gilmore, if it ever really lost it. (I've never found an explanation of the friendly relationship between Pacific and Sero.) The drive-in spent another couple of decades of quiet life before closing at the end of the 1977 season. Its façade stood for another five years before it was razed for redevelopment. The Grove shopping center occupies the site today.

Pacific / Pico Drive-In

Opened: Sept. 9, 1934

Closed: Oct. 1, 1944

Capacity: 500 cars

Location: On Pico and Westwood boulevards, less than a mile southeast of Route 66.

This place, built by Seth Perkins and opened as "Drive-In Theatre," was only the second permanent drive-in ever built. It was the first to license Richard Hollingshead's patent, and the first to show just how successful a drive-in could be. Whether because of its novelty or from leading the zeitgeist, it played to capacity crowds. The corporation that owned it was headed by Guy Douthwaite, and also included Chester Black and Charlie Caballero.

One problem emerged almost immediately. Hollingshead never invented individual car speakers. His

As the only drive-in in town (and west of New Jersey, for that matter), the Pico was initially named simply "Drive-In Theatre." Photo from the Ernest Marquez Collection, The Huntington Library, San Marino, California.

This shot might have been of the Pico's opening night, given all the searchlights in front and the absence of any speakers near the cars. Photo from the "Dick" Whittington Studio Collection of Negatives and Photographs, The Huntington Library, San Marino, California.

first drive-in used a few loudspeakers to blast the viewing field and beyond, and so did this one when it opened. That might have been okay in rural New Jersey, but Los Angeles wouldn't stand for it. By December, City Attorney Ray Chesebro started talking about banning such loudspeakers, and the city passed such an ordinance in February 1935. In March, Douthwaite was arrested. Two officers testified at a trial in June that they could hear the movie a mile and a half from the drive-in. Douthwaite was convicted, but the judge suspended sentence on the condition that he not commit a similar offense for a year. The drive-in was closed.

Forced to come up with a solution, Douthwaite invented individual car speakers. They were strung in front of the car ramps, and each was attached to a front radiator. The drive-in reopened just a few weeks after it closed. Douthwaite apparently stayed out of jail, running

The solution to the screen-mounted loudspeaker problem was individual speakers for every car. They were attached to the front grill, and the sound still wasn't that great. Photo from the California Historical Society via the University of Southern California, Libraries.

the drive-in for another year before resigning for health reasons in late 1936. Black took over operation of what was soon called the Pico Drive-In. (Some references to the drive-in called it the Pacific, but it advertised as the Pico.)

Black was a promoter, arranging ads attached to Borden milk and cream bottles, and donating radios to two lucky patrons in a stunt that *Boxoffice* called "the first giveaway ever staged at a drive-in theatre." In 1940, the company incorporated into what would later become Pacific Drive-In Theaters.

In 1944, the Pico faced a problem it couldn't beat. After just 10 years of operation, its lease was canceled in favor of a housing project. (A shopping mall sits there today.) With enough advance notice, the owners bought 10 acres at Olympic and Bundy where they could build a new drive-in. During the 1944-45 off-season, they did just that, as you'll see in the next entry.

Olympic Drive-In

Opened: April 4, 1945

Closed: Oct. 14, 1973

Capacity: 775 cars

Location: On Olympic Boulevard at Bundy Drive, less than a mile southeast of Route 66.

Pacific Drive-Ins had learned a few lessons from its Pico Drive-In two miles up the road. When it was forced to start from scratch, it made the Olympic a little larger and gave it state-of-the-art RCA in-car speakers. Its screen was probably a little larger – 40x50 feet. Its stage, which it called the "largest in the world," was moved from the Pico at a cost of $8000. Chester Black and Charlie Caballero were still around, joined by Jack Tingle and Guy Gunderson.

In the late 1940s, drive-in competition blossomed, and the Olympic remodeled. It added a playground in 1950, upgraded its speakers, and enlarged its rest rooms. In 1951, it replaced the neon letters on the back of its screen tower with a mural of surfers.

This photo from the May 1946 *Motion Picture Herald* showed the Olympic at night, with its standalone marquee in the foreground and the neon sign on its screen tower behind it.

The Olympic lived the quiet life as one of the most successful Pacific-owned drive-ins for the next few decades. A scene in the 1960 Bob Hope movie *The Facts of*

Life gave viewers a good look at the drive-in. In the end, it closed for the same reason most urban drive-ins closed – skyrocketing land values. Pacific sold the Olympic to a Cadillac dealer in 1973 for $3 million, worth about $18 million in 2021 dollars. Dealers sold cars on the old drive-in site for 40 years. Today that corner is transitioning to the West Edge retail-office-apartment complex.

In 1947, the Olympic still had plenty of undeveloped land behind it. Photo © HistoricAerials.com, used by permission.

Pacific Drive-Ins replaced the plain block neon at the back of the Olympic's screen tower with a larger "Olympic" in neon script and a mural of surfers. 1977 photo by John Margolies, Roadside America photograph archive (1972-2008), Library of Congress, Prints and Photographs Division.

The Santa Monica Pier marks the western end of Route 66. Photo © littleny/Depositphotos.com.

The End

We've reached the end of our journey past over 100 drive-in theaters, most of them sadly lost to history. I hope you enjoyed the ride.

Let me close with a reminder that at least one "fact" in this book will probably turn out to be wrong, and much more information is simply absent. That's where you come in. If you know a cousin or an uncle who used to be a projectionist and has a stack of old newspaper clippings, ask about sharing copies of them. If your town's drive-in is missing details or anecdotes, visit your library to check local newspapers, bound in volumes or on microfilm.

When you have something good to add, please drop me a line at Route66@carload.com. Together, we can keep the memories alive of both our treasured outdoor theaters and the Mother Road that connected them.

Bonus Gallery

Lucky you! Here are a few extra photos that are worth sharing with you, but which I couldn't quite squeeze into any particular chapter.

Here are two 2019 photos by the author. Above, I tried to get a hint of sunset while capturing both of the screens in this photo, too wide to fit in the Barstow CA Skyline entry. Below, a look through a hole in the wire fence at the Sunset in Albuquerque NM showed a physical plant in better shape than some active drive-ins I've seen. Since those pictures were taken, the Skyline has remained unchanged, but the Sunset razed almost everything but the screen.

There are so many great books about the history of Route 66 that I felt a little embarrassed covering it, even briefly. If I had more room, I'd add more photos like these two. Above, a sign in Arizona, undated photo © Helena Bilkova | Dreamstime.com. Below, my very favorite source for chili dogs, the Dog House (with wagging neon tail) in Albuquerque NM, 2011 photo by PerryPlanet.

Bonus Gallery

Here are two more photos from the John Margolies Roadside America photograph archive (1972-2008), Library of Congress, Prints and Photographs Division. Above, the other side of the Airway sign in St. Ann MO. Below, another angle of the original Tascosa screen tower, Amarillo TX.

Finally, two more of my 2021 pictures of the 66 Drive-In in Carthage MO, a truly great place for taking photos. Above, the full spread of its playground equipment, temporarily closed because of pandemic restrictions. Below, one last look at the 66 sign's neon colors as sunset turned to twilight.

Acknowledgments

In putting this book together, I felt like a bricklayer, taking the materials that so many helpers generously provided and just trying to build them straight.

There are so many contributors to thank that I'm sure I'll miss at least one, but I'll do my best.

First, special thanks to Nathan McDonald for allowing me to use a photo of his magnificent 66 Drive-In on the cover. I also want to thank:

The Albuquerque Museum, for providing some stunning early photos of their drive-ins.

Mary Billington and everyone at the Baxter County (KS) Heritage Center for their generous assistance.

Ken Bogren of Route66Times.com, for allowing me to use his photo of the remains of Carthage MO's Sunset.

Joe Bob Briggs, patron saint of drive-in writers and America's foremost drive-in movie critic.

The Dydzak family, for verifying their brief ownership of the Twin Drive-In of Amarillo TX.

The Edmond (OK) Historical Society & Museum, which dug into the inscrutable history of its drive-ins.

Bill Eichelberger, for his Azusa Foothill photo.

Ron Enderland at MiamiHistory.net for his photo of the Tri-State Drive-In.

Steve Fitch, an amazing photographer and generous supporter of my work.

John Gateley, for allowing me to use his stark Joshua Drive-In photo.

Carole Goggin, who works at the Rolla branch of the State Historical Society of Missouri, for tracking down clippings and helping to prove negatives.

Carol M. Highsmith, for continuing to take roadside pictures and donating them to the Library of Congress.

HistoricAerials.com, a great online resource.

The Huntington Library, which provided amazing historic photos of the Pico/Pacific Drive-In.

The Internet Archive (archive.org), which hosts trade publications and other material of interest to researchers, plus lots of fun movies, books, music, and more.

Scott Jentsch of BigScreen Cinema Guide (www.bigscreen.com), another fine movie theater site.

Chris Larson of the Buckeye AZ Library, for details about the second Western Star Drive-In.

Elisa Leonelli, for taking pictures of so many southern California drive-ins in the late 1970s, then generously allowing me to include some of them here.

John Margolies, who took so many great pictures of roadside Americana, then left them for us all to enjoy.

Gary Mays and everyone at the Webster County MO Historical Museum in Marshfield for all their work.

The Missouri State Archives, which supplied dozens of great old Missouri Highway Department photos for me to look through and use here.

The Navajo County Historical Society in Holbrook AZ, which passed along their 66's Drive-In's final ads.

The Needles (CA) Regional Museum, which helped track down the only photo of that city's drive-in.

The New Mexico State Library, for all sorts of research.

Northern Arizona University's Cline Library, for making its medium-resolution images freely available.

The Oklahoma Historical Society, which researched the stories of the Fair Park and Bearcat drive-ins for me.

Ken Roe and everyone at CinemaTreasures.org, an excellent repository of theater history.

Acknowledgements

Don Sporleder of Davenport OK and the Museum of Pioneer History in Chandler for tracking down the Rig.

Springfield IL's Lincoln Library and its Sangamon Valley Collection.

The Tulsa Historical Society and Museum, which also published *Tulsa Movie Theaters* (2021), another great history book full of photos.

Steve Walser, for allowing me to use his amazing photo of the Bel-Air sign in Pontoon Beach IL.

Marty Yawnick at Lifeinlofi.com, for letting me use his photo of the shell of the Trail Drive-In of Athens TX.

And my wife, Anita, for riding shotgun on my photography runs, and my whole family for their support and encouragement.

The 66 shield on the book spine is © zager / Depositphotos.com. State chapter heading graphics are all © TeddyandMia / Depositphotos.com.
The front cover was assembled by the author from the following ingredients:
    Neon Green Light Alphabet Vector Font © Epifantsev / Depositphotos.com.
    Deep space © titoOnz / Depositphotos.com.
    Route 66 Sign © zager / Depositphotos.com.
    Author's 2021 photo of the 66 Drive-In, Carthage MO.

Here's a particularly important acknowledgment:
Several of the photos in this book were licensed through Creative Commons. Some used CC 2.0:
CC 2.0 https://creativecommons.org/licenses/by/2.0/
and some used CC 3.0:
CC 3.0 https://creativecommons.org/licenses/by/3.0/
Thanks to all of you for sharing. You can find a few dozen of my drive-in photos with CC 2.0 licensing on Flickr here:
https://www.flickr.com/photos/carload/

Here are the CC-licensed photos in this book, in order, with links to their originals:

Illinois
Bel-Air Drive-In (Cicero) photo posted by DarkstarMike via CinemaTreasures.org. CC 3.0 http://cinematreasures.org/theaters/4529/photos/75675

66 Drive-In (Countryside) photos posted by salc65 via CinemaTreasures.org. CC 3.0
http://cinematreasures.org/theaters/5662/photos/205847
http://cinematreasures.org/theaters/5662/photos/205848

Missouri
Broadway Drive-In photo posted by MitchWolf via CinemaTreasures.org. CC 3.0 http://cinematreasures.org/theaters/8629/photos/302850

Webb City sign photo posted by moviejs1944 via CinemaTreasures.org. CC 3.0 http://cinematreasures.org/theaters/40250/photos/239175

Oklahoma
Sooner sign photo posted by Chris1982 via CinemaTreasures.org. CC 3.0 http://cinematreasures.org/theaters/11892/photos/100023

Davenport Rig matchbook posted by ScreenTower via CinemaTreasures.org. CC 3.0 http://cinematreasures.org/theaters/28693/photos/117119

New Mexico
Abuquerque 66 night neon photo posted by Michigandriveins.com via CinemaTreasures.org. CC 3.0 http://cinematreasures.org/theaters/56631/photos/285078

Grants Sahara and Milan Trails photos posted by Nlister via CinemaTreasures.org. CC 3.0
http://cinematreasures.org/theaters/54803/photos/231516
http://cinematreasures.org/theaters/48641/photos/231510

El Trovatore Motel photo posted by Jerry Huddleston on Flickr. CC 2.0
https://www.flickr.com/photos/9265232@N04/33638760532

El Rancho Hotel photo posted by Nicholas Jones on Flickr. CC 2.0
https://www.flickr.com/photos/34654604@N08/6958743656

Blue Swallow Motel photo posted by Harry Pherson on Flickr. CC 2.0
https://www.flickr.com/photos/32559259@N06/9353910597

California
Valley sign photo posted by dallasmovietheaters via CinemaTreasures.org. CC 3.0 http://cinematreasures.org/theaters/24865/photos/352095

Edwards sign photo posted by ChrisB via CinemaTreasures.org. CC 3.0 http://cinematreasures.org/theaters/6411/photos/75789

Index

270 Drive-In 57
4-Screen Drive-In 71-73
40 Drive-In 151-154
11th Street Drive-In 118-120
14 Flags Drive-In 138
19 Drive-In 82-84
66 Drive-In
 (Albuquerque NM) 201-203
66 Drive-In (Carthage MO)
 98-100, 112, 272
66 Drive-In
 (Countryside IL) 26-27
66 Drive-In
 (Elk City OK) 158-159
66 Drive-In
 (Holbrook AZ) 219-220
66 Drive-In
 (Oklahoma City OK) 138-139
66 Drive-In
 (Springfield IL) 41-43
66 Park-In
 (Crestwood MO) 62-64
66 West Twin Drive-In
 (Weatherford OK) 151-154
77 Drive-In 138, 142
88 Drive-In 164

Admiral Twin Drive-In 122-123
Airline Drive-In 138
Airview Drive-In 120-121
Airway Drive-In
 (St. Ann MO) 69-71, 271
Albuquerque NM 107-108,
 188-203, 214, 215, 269, 270
Albuquerque 6 Drive-In 188
Albuquerque Theaters 196, 202
All-States Theatres
 189, 191, 195, 196
Alumbaugh, Wes 99
Amarillo TX 169-180, 271
Amboy CA 212
Anchorage AK 108
Anderson, Arnold and Jack 246
Apache Drive-In 124-125
Arcadia CA 254-256
Armino, D. 201
Armstrong, George 202
Arthur Enterprises 73
Autoscopes 105-108
Auto-Vu Drive-In 217
Avery, Cyrus 15-16, 91, 118
Azusa CA 250-251
Azusa Foothill Drive-In 250-251

Baccus, Marsha 131
Balaban, Harry and Elmer 28, 29
Balch, William Glenn 261
Baldock, Jack 236-237
Balsam Drive-In 238-239
Bar-Len Drive-In 234-236

Barnet, James 136
Barstow CA 231-233, 269
Barton, Olen 89
Barton, R. Lewis, Theatres
 139, 142, 143, 147-148, 150
Bates, Norman 27
Baxter Springs KS 109-111
Beacon Theatres 245
Bearcat Drive-In 159-161
Bearden, Wendell Oren
 169-170, 174, 180
Bel-Air Drive-In
 (Cicero IL) 23-25
Bel-Air Drive-In
 (Fontana CA) 244-245
Bel-Air Drive-In
 (Pontoon Beach IL) 49-50
Bel-Air Drive-In
 (Romeoville IL) 28-29
Bellaire Drive-In
 (Tulsa OK) 128-129
Belmont Amusement Corp. 23
Bennis Auto Vue Drive-In 35-36
Bennis, Steve 35-36
Berman, Lou 252
Bethany OK 148-150
Bethel, R. 90
Big Sky Drive-In 252-253
Black, Chester 263, 265, 266
Blocker, John 180
Bloomington IL 33-34
Bloomington Drive-In 33-34
Blue, Alex 123
Bowden, Jake 118
Boyter, Athel 166
Bradfield, William 98-99, 101
Bridgeton MO 67-68
Briggs, Joe Bob 114, 232
Brister, Dale 159
Bristow OK 132-134
Broadway Drive-In 58-60
Brout, R. Benedict 232
Buckeye AZ 218
Buffalo MO 106-107
Burke Enterprises 144
Burns, Rhett Butler 175-176
Butler, Clifford and Helen
 192-193
Butler, Marlin 193-194, 200
Byrd, Al 37

Caballero, Charlie 263, 266
Cactus Drive-In 196-197
Camden NJ 3, 4
Canal Drive-In 185-186
Cantrell, Dwight 91
Caporal, George 142
Capri Drive-In 118
Carlton, Cecil 248
Carmike 114, 118, 153, 159

Carney, Rowe 83, 84-86
Cars (2006 movie) 22, 217, 226
Carthage MO 96-100, 112, 272
Cave City KY 226
Centinela Drive-In 259
Chain of Rocks Bridge
 20, 55-56, 57
Chaney, Sheldon "Red" 19
Cherokee Drive-In 109
Chesebro, Marvin 259-260
Chesebro, Ray 260, 264
Cicero IL 23-25
Cinema 66 Drive-In 138-139
Cinema 70 Drive-In 146-147
Cinema C Drive-In 147-148
Cinema-Surf Club 241
Cinemark 239
Circle Autoscope 107-108
Circle Drive-In 147-148
Circle, Harry 147
Claremore OK 117-118
Clinton OK 156-157
Clinton Drive-In 156-157
Collins, George 29
Collinsville IL 51-52
Comet Theatres 257
Commonwealth Theatres
 86, 87-88, 92, 93-94, 95,
 103, 104-105, 186, 194,
 196, 200, 203, 208-209
Congdon, Byron "Bud" 240-241
Conrad, R. E. 141
Contreras, Adrian and Arturo
 31
Coppola, Frances Ford 123
Countryside IL 26-27
County Drive-In 183-185
Crest Drive-In 102-103
Crestwood MO 61-64
Crossroads Company 174-175
Crouch, Edward "E. R." 230-231
Cuba MO 82-84

Danz, John 258
Davenport OK 134-135
Derby Drive-In 167-169
Des Peres MO 64-67
Dickinson Theatres
 99, 101-102, 110-111, 155
Dobson, Garland 160-161
Dollison, Lester
 172-173, 187-188
Double Drive-In 23, 24
Doughwaite, Guy 263-264
Doyle, Leroy 174
Drielsma, J. Arthur 252
Drum, Jack 253
Duarte CA 252-253
Duke City Drive-In 194-195
Dydzak, Joseph 177

East St. Louis IL 52-54
East St. Louis Drive-In 52
Echols, Connie 82
Edmond OK 135-138
Edmond Drive-In 136
Edmondson, Lillie 160
Edwards Drive-In 254-256
Edwards Theatres 250, 254-256
El Reno OK 150-153
El Reno Drive-In 150-153
Electric Dusk Drive-In 259
Elk City OK 6, 158-159
Entertainment Centers of America 238, 239
Erick OK 159-161
Fagan, John 172, 176-177, 178-179
Fair Park Drive-In 139-141
Falcon Drive-In 51-52
Falls Drive-In 180
Falls, Horace 139-140
Family Theatres 125
Fantastic Caverns 57
Farrell, Bob 53
Ferris, Charles and Maurice 146
Ferris Enterprises 139, 146
Flagstaff AZ 223-224
Flexer, David 62-63
Florissant MO 1
Fontana CA 243-245
Foothill Drive-In 242-243
Forbes, Dave 87
Ford, Claude 260
Forte, John 249
Fossell, George 194
Four-Screen Drive-In 71-73
Fox West Coast 248
French Village Drive-In 52
Friedman, David 30
Frisina Amusement Company 39-40, 45-46
Frontier Theatres 186, 194, 196, 203, 208
Galaxy Theatres 144
Gallup NM 207-211, 216
Gamble, Ted 244
Gayle, Brian 155
General Cinema 27, 70, 123
General Drive-In 27
George, Robert 155
Gibson, Blanche 150-152
Gilmore Drive-In 260-262
Glendale AZ 13
Goodman, Mark 99-100
Graham, Hugh 81
Grand Canyon 19
Grand Canyon Caverns 19
Grande Drive-In 80-82
Grants NM 204-205
Gray, Opal 152
Greater Oklahoma City Amusements 148, 150
Green Meadows Drive-In 43-45

Griffing, Tom 189, 191, 194-195
Griffith, Henry 196
Griffith, L. C. 156
Griffith Theatres 113, 119, 127, 130, 151, 153, 156, 159, 196
Gulf States Theatres 142, 143, 146, 150
Gunderson, Guy 266
Guthrie, Lamar 160-161
Halberg, Carl and Phyllis 198-199, 200
Hale, Doug 154
Halloway, Henry 69
Harbor Drive-In 259
Hardgrave, Harry 123
Hargis, Earl 89
Harris, M. A. 137
Hartstein, Herbert 68
Harvey, Gene 233
Hastings Drive-In 257-258
Heritage Theatres 147
Hewitt, Leonard 32
Hillcrest Drive-In 138
Hilltop Drive-In 29-31
Hi-M Drive-In 91
Hi-Way 66 Drive-In 118-120
Hoese, Robert H. 257
Holbrook AZ 215, 217-220, 226-228
Holiday Drive-In (Overland MO) 74-76
Holiday Drive-In (Springfield MO) 92-93
Hollingshead Jr., Richard 3, 4, 63, 263
Hollywood Theatres 102
Holmes, Freeman 133
Holt, O. D. 133
Honda Project Drive-In 13, 233
Horne, Howard 167
Houston TX 108
Hubble, Edwin 90
Hull, Jack and Jimmy 137
Hurley, Milas 185-186
I-44 Drive-In 78-79
Jablonow, Louis 49, 58, 74
Jacobs, Larry 249-250
Jaeger, J. 82
Jennings MO 60-61
Joliet IL 29-31
Joliet View Corp. 30
Jones, Ted 238
Joplin MO 102-105, 107
Joseph, Irwin 30
Kaimann, Clarence 60-61
Kante Group 132
Karonis, Peter 33-34
Katsky, Bill 253
Kennedy, F. 90
Kent, Keith 190

Kerasotes Theatres 32-33, 34, 40-43
King, Jim 224
Kingman AZ 212, 224-226
Knight, Doug 44-45
Knight, George and Audrey 44
Knudson, David 21
Komm Theaters 49-50, 51, 53-54, 58, 74
Krueger, Paul 77
Krueger, Ronald Paul 61, 77-78
L&M Management 29, 31
La Verna CA 247-250
Lake Air Drive-In 148-150
Lally, Thomas E. 32
Lang Theatre Company 225
Lariat Drive-In 116-117
Larsen, Howard 101
Lawler, Ralph 38
Lebanon MO 88-90, 213, 214
Lee, S. Charles 254
Leeson, Clyde 96-97
Lenwood CA 234-236
Leonelli, Elisa 241, 246, 253, 255, 261, 262
Levine, Rube 29
Lewis, Charles 227
Lewis, Clifton and Paul 227
Lincoln IL 35-37
Lincoln Drive-In 36-37
Linda Vista Drive-In 188
Litchfield IL 2, 45-46
London, Julie 221
Long, Louis 219
Long, Walter G. 244, 248
Los Angeles CA 258-267
Los Feliz Drive-In 259-260
Lowenstein, Harry 156
Lyons, Patrick "P. K." 235
M & R Theaters 24
Malone, J. 131
Manchester Drive-In 65-67, 93
Mann Theatres 248
Maples, Christopher 93
Margolies, John 34, 63, 170-171, 173, 179, 180-181, 197, 228, 249, 267, 271
Marks, Raymond 24
Marshall, W. T. 193
Marshfield MO 90-91
Martin Theatres 114, 117, 153, 157
Mason, Doug 190
Mathis, John 82
McCoy, Hazel 137
McDonald, Nathan 100
McDonald, Paul 177
McDowell, Roy 207
McFarland, Charles B. 148-150
McGhee, Walter D. 5
McKee, W. H. 37
McLean TX 166-169
Meier, Adolph and Zeta 82-83

Index 279

Meramec Caverns 19, 57, 79
Merrick, Rex 170
Miami OK 113-115
Mid America Theatres 40, 44, 46, 50, 51-52, 58, 76
Midwest Drive-In Theatres 69
Milan NM 206-207
Mills, William 63
Mini Drive-In 107-108
Mini 5 Drive-In 88
Minturn CO 14
Mission Drive-In 245
Modernaire Drive-In 122-123
Montclair CA 245-247
Moonlight Drive-In 88
Moonlight Movies System 242
Morley, Fred 200
Morley, Robert 198
Mounds Drive-In 51-52
Mount Olive IL 47-48
Mt. Baldy Drive-In 248-250
Mt. Elden Drive-In 223-224
Mt. Vernon Drive-In 240-241
Murray, Ken Gordon 31-32
Nace, Harry 219, 221-222, 223, 225
Nagle, William 208, 210-211
National General 248
National Production Authority 7, 137, 174, 200, 210
National Theatres & TV 248
N'eastern 66 Drive-In 138-139
Needles CA 229-231
Nethery, W. J. 147
New Grande Investment Corp. 81
No Name Drive-In 183-185
North Drive-In 60-61
North Penn Twin Drive-In 142-144
Northern Arizona Theatres 223-224
Northside Drive-In 188
Northwest Highway Drive-In 141-142
Norton, Lee 81
O'Donnell, James 136
Odom Drive-In 138, 141
Odorizzi, Louis 47-48
Oldknow, William 246
Olympic Drive-In 266-267
O'Keefe, Al 244
Oklahoma Cinema Theatres 146
Oklahoma City OK 138-148
Olympic Drive-In (Los Angeles CA) 266-267
Olympic Drive-In (Pagedale MO) 57
Onondaga Cave 57
Ontario Neon 246
Ornelas, Saul 31
Overland MO 74-76
Owen, Harold 90-91
Pacific Drive-In 263-265
Pacific Drive-In Theatres 241, 243, 245, 253, 255, 262, 265, 266-267
Page, Amos 160, 168
Page, Madge 168
Painted Desert 18
Palo-Duro Drive-In 178-179
Parker, A. Ray 59-60, 67-68
Parsons Drive-In 109
Pasadena CA 256-258
Pastrovich, Mike and Debbie 46
Pastrovich, Nick and Mindy 46
Paul, Norman and Del 46
Peerless Theaters 141-142
Perkins, Seth 263
Peterson, George 38
Petrified Forest 19
Phil-Kron Drive-In 33-34
Phillips, Bob 168
Phillips, Kenneth 32, 33-34
Pico Drive-In 263-265
Pimes Company 51
Pioneer Drive-In 165-166
Pirate Drive-In 132-134
Playgrounds 7, 27, 66, 75, 101, 111-112, 121, 126, 144, 164, 266
Pontiac IL 31-33
Pontiac Drive-In 31-33
Pontoon Beach IL 49-50
Powell, James R. 54
Prickett, Ken 27
Project Drive-In 13
Projectors, digital 12-14
Providence RI 5
Queen City Twin Drive-In 91
Radio sound 10, 11, 239
Randall, Jim 103
Redford, Frank 226-227
Rialto CA 242-243
Richland WA 108
Rig Drive-In 134-135
Riverside Drive-In 127-128
Riviera Drive-In 138
RKO 76
Robb, Henry 123
Rock Road Drive-In 57
Rodkey, Larry 232-233
Rolla MO 84-86
Rolla Drive-In 84-86
Rogers-Kante, Joni 132
Rogers, Will 18-19, 117
Rogers Drive-In 117-118
Ronnie's Drive-In 76-78
Rosenfeld, Martin & Richard 24
Roupe, Edward 136
Route 25 Drive-In 198-199
Route 66 Drive-In 43-45
Sahara Drive-In 204-205
Salcido, Arthur 184
San Bernardino CA 19, 226, 228, 240-241
San Jose Drive-In 198-199
Sand Springs Drive-In 118
Sands Drive-In 229-231
Sanford, Bob 208
Santa Fe NM 1
Santa Rosa NM 186-188
Santee Drive-In 249
Sappington MO 76-78
Sapulpa OK 129-132
Sayetta, Sidney 69-70
Shaffer, Tommy 81
Schmidt, Lloyd 90-91
Schwartz, Abe 80-81
Seligman AZ 216
Sero Amusement 198, 200, 246, 261-262
Shamrock TX 165-166
Shanbour, Farris 146-147
Sheridan Drive-In 125-126
Shimbach, Jerry 30
Shop City Drive-In 52-54
Shull, Randy 233
Shuttee, Walter 150-152
Siebenman, Ted 81
Silver Dollar Twin Drive-In 188
Sikes, Joseph 38-39
Simpson, Henry 132-133
Sinnett, Rick 151, 153
Ski-Hi Drive-In 89-90
Skyline Drive-In (Barstow CA) 231-233, 269
Skyline Drive-In (Bridgeton MO) 67-68
Skyline Drive-In (Marshfield MO) 90-91
Skyline Drive-In (Tulsa OK) 118
Sky-Ranch Drive-In 187-188
Sky View Drive-In (Litchfield IL) 2, 45-46
Skyview Drive-In (Oklahoma City OK) 138
Skyway Drive-In 172-173
Slocum, E. R. "Red" 151-153
Slusher, Waldo V. 184
Sylvester, Woodie 153
Smith, Blake 123
Smith, Phillip 26, 65, 69
Smith, Preston 169
Smith, Richard D. 123
Smith, Tom 105-108
Snow, John Hasten 183-184
Snyder, L. E. (Earl) 122-123, 124-125
Sooner Drive-In 113-115
South Twin Drive-In 57
Southwestern Theaters 139
Speakers, external 65, 91, 119, 263-264
Speakers, in-car 5, 6, 152, 168, 266
Spearman, C. H. 137
Spectro 146
Spreng, Don and Susan 83-84

Spreng, Karen	84	
Springdale AR	108	
Springfield IL	19, 38-45	
Springfield (IL) Drive-In	38-40	
Springfield MO	18, 19, 91-95	
Springfield (MO) Drive-In	93-94, 111	
Squaw Drive-In	150-153	
St. Ann MO	69-73, 271	
St. Ann 4-Screen Drive-In	71-73	
St. Louis MO	57-60	
St. Louis Amusement Co.	72	
St. Robert MO	86-88	
Star Chief Drive-In	31-33	
Star Drive-In (Albuquerque NM)	188	
Star Drive-In (Montrose CO)	161	
Stein, Louis	109	
Sterling Theatres	258	
Stiver, Marvin	73	
Stockman, Tom	79	
Stribling, Joe	134-135	
Stromme, Richard	134	
Sullivan MO	79-82	
Sullivan, Odom Farrell	141	
Sullivan Theatres	142	
Sundown Drive-In (Edmond OK)	137-138	
Sunset Drive-In (Albuquerque)	200-201, 269	
Sunset Drive-In (Amarillo TX)	179-180	
Sunset Drive-In (Carthage MO)	96-97	
Sunset Drive-In (Mount Olive IL)	47-48	
Sunset Drive-In (Muskogee OK)	136	
Sunset Drive-In (Springfield MO)	94-95	
Taft, Sam	93	
Tascosa Drive-In	173-176, 271	
Tee-Pee Drive-In	129-132	
Terrace Drive-In	188-190	
Tesuque Drive-In	192-194	
Texas National Theaters	203	
Tharp, Twyla	242-243	
Tharp, William	242-243	
Theatre Enterprises	210	
Theatre Operators	207	
Thomas, Leo and Lydia	138-139	
Thompson, Howard	89	
Thunderbird Drive-In	57-58	
Tingle, Jack	266	
Tonto Drive-In	220-222	
Trail Drive-In (Amarillo TX)	169-172	
Trail Drive-In (Athens TX)	182	
Tri-C Drive-In	198-199	
Tri-State Drive-In (Joplin MO)	104-105	
Tri-State Drive-In (Miami OK)	113-114	
Troup, Bobby	18, 221	
Tucker, George	196, 200	
Tucumcari NM	183-186, 213, 216	
Tulsa OK	118-129, 213	
Turner, Ron	136	
Twilight Gardens Drive-In	144-145	
Twilite Drive-In	109-111	
Twin Drive-In (Amarillo TX)	176-177	
Twin Drive-In (Springfield IL)	40-41	
Twin-Vue Drive-In	259	
Tyler, Cal	246	
Unger, Earle E.	193	
Union NJ	4	
Urbana MO	105, 107	
U.S. TRAD	108	
Valley Drive-In	245-247	
Valley Park MO	78-79	
Victorville CA	236-239	
Victory Drive-In	259	
Video Independent Theatres	113-115, 116-117, 117-118,119-120, 121, 126, 127, 130, 144, 152, 153, 156-157, 189, 191-192, 195	
Vinita OK	115-117	
Wagner, Thomas I.	28	
Walling, Harry	132	
Walter, Bob	104-105	
Waugh, Bruce	210	
Waynesville MO	87	
Weatherford OK	151-154	
Webb City MO	100-102	
Webb City Drive-In	101-102	
Wehrenberg, Fred	60, 63, 76	
Wehrenberg Theatres	60, 63-64, 70-71, 73, 77-78, 78	
Weisenberg, Charles	172, 176-177, 178-179	
Weseman, R. L.	53	
West, Jerome "J.C."	204-205, 206-207	
Western Amusement Company	230, 232, 235-236, 236-238, 238-239	
Western Outdoor Management	27	
Western Star Drive-In	217-219	
Westside Theatres	225	
WFW Theatres	178	
Whipple, F. C.	221	
Wilhoit, Rush	93	
Wilkins, Chet	246	
Wilkinson, Bill	133	
Wilkinson, Willie	133	
Williams AZ	21	
Williams, Mike	168-169	
Wilson, Eugene	71	
Wilson, Harold	172, 176, 178-179	
Winchester Drive-In	138	
Winslow AZ	220-222	
Wolfenbarger, Dan	154, 166	
Woodcock, Myron	81	
Woodlane Drive-In	86-88	
Woodruff, John	91	
Woodstock Drive-In	136	
Worley, J. Seibert	165-166	
Wyoming Drive-In	191-192	
Yessler, Bertha	184	
Yessler, Loren	184-185	
Young, Elizabeth	217	
Young, Robert	217-219	
Youngblood, William & F. B.	37	
Yucca Drive-In (Clovis NM)	180	
Yucca Drive-In (Gallup NM)	210-211	
Zuni Drive-In	208-209	

About the author

Michael Kilgore is the webmaster of Carload.com, a drive-in theater information source since 1998. He has been recognized for his work by the Library of Congress. Previously, he was a writer and editor for the *Kansas City Star* and other newspapers. He also wrote *Drive-Ins of Route 66 (first edition)* and *Drive-Ins of Colorado*.

www.ingramcontent.com/pod-product-compliance
Lightning Source LLC
Chambersburg PA
CBHW071954070526
44583CB00015B/1193